Cornelius J. Smal is the author of the multi-language inspirational adventure book series, *The Adventures of Sparky*. All his books are true stories based on his adventures and life experiences. He lives in Cape Town, South Africa, and loves great adventure, extreme sports and traveling. He also loves inspiring people with his passion for entertaining people, acting, and playing the piano. He studied BA Drama at the University of Pretoria and Education, through the University of South Africa.

During his childhood, Cornelius and Nils Holgerson could have been the same character. In short, he was always a good-natured naughty little 'Dennis the menace' type of boy. From a young age, his mother couldn't use enough soap to wash that crimson African farm soil out of his lily blonde hair. Cornelius had the perfect childhood living on a farm that any city boy could only dream about. Ample space, beautiful bushveld, and a vegetable garden, and with that unprecedented freedom, his great love for nature was born.

For my dad, Pieter.

Thank you for your never-ending wisdom and for being the rock of our family. You are always willing to support my dreams and endeavors, and always willing to selflessly bail me out when my stubbornness faces expensive life lessons.

My mom, Elmine.

Thank you for being a wonderful selfless mom and always giving your best for our family. Your prayers are always incredibly heartfelt.

My brothers.

Christiaan, for inspiring me to breathe life into my testimony and Pieter for teaching me to stand up for myself.

My late doggies Mielies (Corn) and Spikkels (Spots). Thank you for your unconditional love, you are truly missed.

Cornelius J. Smal

KNYSNA FOREST

A True Epic Survival Story

AUSTIN MACAULEY PUBLISHERS™

LONDON • CAMBRIDGE • NEW YORK • SHARJAH

Ordering Information
Quantity sales: Special discounts are available on quantity purchases by corporations, associations, and others. For details, contact the publisher at the address below.

Publisher's Cataloging-in-Publication data
Smal, Cornelius J.
Knysna Forest

ISBN 9798886935721 (Paperback)
ISBN 9798886935738 (Hardback)
ISBN 9798886935752 (ePub e-book)
ISBN 9798886935745 (Audiobook)

Library of Congress Control Number: 2023919161

www.austinmacauley.com/us

First Published 2024
Austin Macauley Publishers LLC
40 Wall Street, 33rd Floor, Suite 3302
New York, NY 10005
USA

mail-usa@austinmacauley.com
+1 (646) 5125767

I would like to express my gratitude to Mrs. Wasserman, Nieuwoudt, Grobler, Rustenburg High School, and the grade eleven group of 2003 who invited me on the hike. Everyone who contributed to the great search, and all who interceded with prayers. The experience of a lifetime not only changed my life and strengthened me, but also prepared me for bigger adventures that occurred later in my life. I would also like to congratulate you on your brave choice to be part of this phenomenal life-changing epic story of survival. Enjoy the epic adventure.

Table of Contents

Why Should You Read This Book?

This is my true account of survival in the majestic Knysna forest. Knysna Forest is not a colorful fictional tale but born out of an actual miraculous survival experience in 2003, when I should have died at the age of 19.

What was cut out to be just a wonderful getaway and revitalizing adventure suddenly turned fateful. Stuck in a continuous rollercoaster ride of overwhelming anxiety and rhetorical emotions, a single glimmer of motivation sparked an unprecedented urge to share my testimony with someone, everyone. I had to stay alive, just a little longer, against all odds. But how?

I am infinitely grateful that now, after so many years, you can experience my miracle testimony.

Prologue

Surely this is it, Lord? I do not want to. I cannot, not now! I still have so much to accomplish in my life, Lord. I have yet to meet my dream girl, and I am only nineteen.

The fight against my sanity and the onslaught on my mood are just getting too heavy to bear.

I have so much pain, Lord, I can't take it any longer, I have no more strength, and I am so thirsty.

It is already dusk and this severe monotonous anxiety has long passed my handling point.

How much more, dear Jesus? Help me, I cannot die now. I'm losing my mind, please, Jesus, help me, help me!

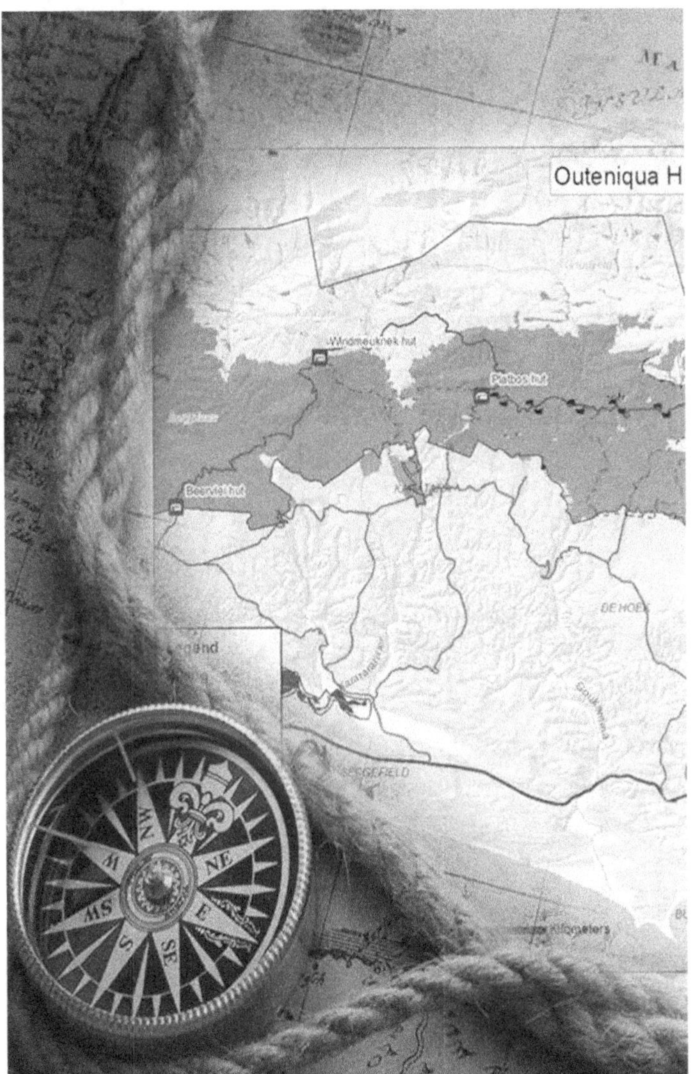

Outeniqua H
Windmeulnek hut
Platbos hut
Beervlei hut
DE HOE
WITGEFELD
Kilometers

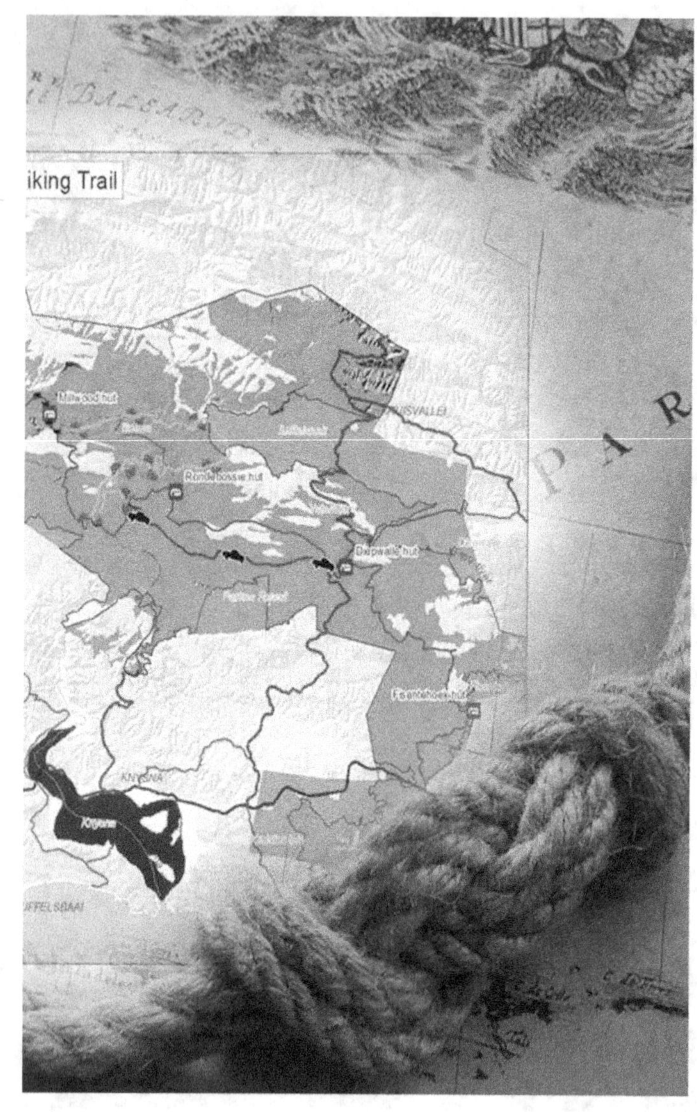
iking Trail
Millwood hut
Rondebosse hut
Diepwalle hut
Paardekops
KNYSNA
Knysna
BUFFELS BAAI
PAR

Introduction

How many lives do you have? If it is not your time, how many times can you cheat death? How many trials can you withstand before you wish it was your time? When you are dangerously close to losing your mind because of the anxiety of being pushed to the limits, becomes too much to bear. What do you do when pain turns into a measure of motivation and salvation, an abstract concept, and a distant dream? Where do you hide from insanity when ghosts break the monotony of loneliness, and you can no longer fight with nature to keep you from its grasp? When the chaos suddenly goes numb, you realize that behind all the hurt, there was an adventure of a lifetime and a life lesson for you to learn.

The First Adventure

My love for the Outeniqua forest began in 2001 when I first hiked the majestically beautiful Knysna Forest with my high school. I have always been a great advocate of living life to the fullest, free of constraints, and couldn't be more excited for our incredible adventure. I didn't need to be invited twice. In preparation for my 'Circles in a forest'-hike in eleventh grade, I took extra food with me just in case I got lost, because I had a slight desire to explore the unknown; getting lost with a cute girl. I planned my entire operation, 'get-lost-together-with-a-cute-girl' carefully.

First, I will talk her scared to death, so she will believe there is no tomorrow, before I, like MacGyver, with my field knowledge, excellent direction, and forestry skills become her knight in shining armor. Ironically, on the very first day, I got a little lost on the way to Platbos, about ten kilometers [±6.5 miles], together with a girl by the name of Chantel Müller.

It was just the way I wanted; a cute girl to scare but only too little time for my master plan to come together. We arrived back at camp with a smile in the rain.

Cupid's misfortune had not sparked my hopes for an innocent 'Knysna-romance,' but more than ever was I motivated to be first every day.

I have always turned everyday activities into passionate, motivating, personal goals, and, as a result, earned my well-deserved nickname *'Speedy'* by Mrs. Grobler.

Every day I purposefully slept an hour later than everyone else, just so that my 'opponents' could get a more significant head start and my challenge for the day got harder and harder. That resulted in me having to run and catch the groups from behind. I think my record still stands at Millwood.

"Last to start and first to finish sixteen kilometers [±10 miles] within three hours," I darted past Mrs. Grobler like *Flash Gordon.*

Day after day, I could take nice long 'victory' showers – if there was hot water I have to add. Nature's sweet scents, beautiful plants, and enchanting sounds every day were like a memorable adventure on its own. Running alone through the beautiful forest was an absolutely fulfilling and almost surreal experience. I filled my mind with thousands of new stories every day thinking that I could entice my 'underprivileged' friends with dedication every night.

They hung on every word I spoke, and stories about my past adventures dripped like honey from my lips. All the chatter I might have missed out on during the day, I caught up one thousand percent at night.

Undauntedly, one night I told a group of girls about my 'massage course' that I enrolled in when I was in Sydney, Australia.

Immediately Sparky was promoted to the 'Knysna masseuse.' In all honesty, all I did was merely borrow some techniques with my eyes on how one Chinese guy inspiringly massaged girl after girl at a shopping center.

It was absolutely an experience when my white lie allowed me to massage all their sore muscles. Even though no one returned the favor to my spastic back, it was still worth it. It was such a blessing to see everyone laugh so joyfully. Instantaneously I got promoted to the alpha male, the woodcutting boss, the fire maker, snake catcher, comedian, 'Dr. Phil,' and even the guru of things I have not yet heard of. Sparky was their hero.

It was undoubtedly one of the most memorable adventures of my life. I will not say that the guys didn't get jealous, but no one could hold it against good-old beloved Sparky. My school days flew by in the blink of an eye and that unforgettable 'Circles in a forest'-hike was only a yearning memory while I was packing fish in the icy cold Northeastern part of Scotland.

The remembrance of my Knysna hike of 2001 caused such a longing to go back to my beloved South Africa. As a result, I impulsively exchanged my United Kingdom money-making excursion for a second Knysna hike. This time with High School Rustenburg's grade elevens of 2003.

With no effort, my brother persuaded Mrs. Grobler and set, I was ready for a second unforgettable adventure.

Chapter 1
Sparky Goes Wild

23 September

"Wake up, Conelius, wake up, the bus will leave you!"

I am woken with an intense loving motherly smack on the forehead. Similar to that time, I had to get my matric results. Up and about, excited, anxiously against time, I shove the necessary supplies in my backpack so I really don't miss the bus.

"Two-minute noodles, tuna, *Game* energy drink, jelly sweets, three energy chocolate bars…check." I am ready for the Knysna forest with my shortened food list.

"I'll get more food from the group."

I remember the last time we hiked how much food was unnecessarily thrown away by my group to lighten their bags every day. I deliberately packed less food.

On the bus from Cape Town to George, the memory of how I completely looked like a sardine from Cornwall on my way to Scotland made me smile, as well as all the strange times. I carelessly realized that I forgot my flashlight.

'You're the best hiker; deadly, who needs a flashlight, man?' I was reassured.

Because of the experience of growing up on a farm, I developed the gift of always straying my way back to the house and therefore had no worries in the world if I ever really got lost.

'I'll show everybody again, where David buried the roots.' I laughed.

'Oh, last time was so enjoyable!'

All the fond memories of my previous hike captivated me, and I couldn't help yearning back to all my friends from back in the day.

'How will the scholars receive me?' I felt slightly out of place because I invited myself to their 'party' and really did not know what to expect.

"Oh, if they don't welcome me with open arms, I'll just run again," was I, the master self-comforter, and not bothered much with peer pressure games. I realized how much life experience I gained being in the United Kingdom for almost a year, and I could not wait to recharge my batteries after my challenging trip overseas.

Arriving at George, a new teacher from my previous school picked me up and took me to the overnight accommodation one day before the big adventure. When I arrived at the camping ground, I realized that my mind did not play tricks on me, and I was clearly out of place. I decided that their candid hospitality must be a sign that they felt inferior.

"Sparky! Sparky!" Some of my old unjust foes sarcastically belittled me. They were part of the only two percentiles who did not like the most famous, yet not the most popular character of High School Rustenburg. I was the infamous, energetic, and loved by almost all, happy-go-lucky ever so hilarious character called 'Sparky.'

I kept myself too thick-skinned to care and soon blended in with everyone else.

"I'm here for the forest and nothing else!"

Out of the blue, unexpectedly, I notice a cute, mesmerizing mademoiselle.

'Ooh, she looks beautiful.' I immediately summed up that she was much more delicate than the type you could find in the UK.

'Wait, Cornelius!' I tactfully decided that connecting with the group before I approached anyone special would be the best choice.

I spent all day at Hartenbos beach with the other ninety-eight percentiles of pals who appreciated Sparky's silly antics.

As I entertained my new found crowd with all my crazy anecdotes from across the sea, I was entirely in my element.

Soon I realized the contrast between South Africa's sunny golden beaches and warm waves versus England's pebble beaches and icy water. It was incredible to be back.

'No matter what, tomorrow, you will show them how to run this forest.' That personal goal of being first every day blazed within me.

'When people least expect it, I'm at my most dangerous.' I smiled focused.

The lovely day by the beach flew by too quickly, and at least before the butchery was closed, I bought myself a ZAR30 piece of biltong *[beef jerky]*.

'Extra protein when I'm bored with tuna.' I carefully stored my piece of biltong in my backpack.

'Ouch, you burned me, huh?' It was clear that the sun smacked my little '*Pommie*' skin.

As I lay in the darkness, long after everyone was asleep, I could only hear the deep breathing and snoring of some people. I couldn't bring myself to fall asleep because I was far too excited. It reminded me of the time when I was a kid and couldn't fall asleep because I was way too excited about my birthday to start.

My mind started to wander and all I could think about was that breathtaking girl that took my sleep away.

'Oh, stop it Sparky, you're being way too romantic now.' I began to lose myself in thought, thinking of ways to break the ice.

The thought of how much more beautiful everything will be here in nature with her put a smile on my face. Suddenly I heard a scuffle at the bags and I froze.

'What was that?' I tried to understand what it could be.

'What if it was a burglar?' My heart started pounding in my chest as I tried to lie dead still.

'There it is again…no wait, Sparky, you have to do something!' I waited for the perfect moment before going into action.

'But…why didn't my dogs bark? I hope my babies are okay?'

I became more anxious and ready for action. As if someone tested fate, a hand suddenly touched my shoulder.

Without wasting a second, with all my might, I grabbed the shape in the darkness above me.

"Whoa, whoa! Sparky wait…just me, don't hurt me, it's time to wake up." Affirms one scholar that the new day has begun.

'When did I fall asleep?' I lay there for a little while before realizing that I had completely forgotten to charge my unreliable phone.

24 September

It is early morning, and with sand still fresh in my eyes, we were on our way to the hiking trail. The bus soon made a quick stop in Knysna for the last shopping, where I, fortunately, bought a disposable camera and batteries for my CD-Walkman.

[I must add that the fact that the disposable camera survived the rivers and every ordeal to have photos in my book is almost unbelievable.]

'You never know when an opportunity arises where you and that special someone can listen to sweet music together.' I was ready for a possible romantic venture.

Confident that I would find excess food every day, I regrettably decided not to buy extra food and headed back to the bus. At the foot of the mountain, the bus turned off at a broad, gravel dirt road and spiraled up the breathtaking altitude.

'This grandeur must be enjoyed with a special someone, period.'

The beautiful forest ignited something inside me. The dense green treetops that nearly touched the sky were so indescribable that I tried to find out how high it might be.

'Wow, maybe a hundred meters or more?'

The immense heights captivated me. The baboon ropes, millions of plants, all the animal noises, the misty hills, and the picture-perfect, breathtaking paradise of pristine unkempt wonder; I was home.

'Where was I all this time?' I felt the captivating peace flowing over me, knowing with all my heart that I would not exchange South Africa's splendor for all the money that the United Kingdom can offer. The sweet smells of the cold, fresh, clean air almost tangible on my lips made me feel slightly sleepy and annoyed that I lay stratifying all night long.

'Yes, you wanted to be awake until who knows what time, planning how you will beat everyone, and now you are too tired to put words into action.'

'Your nickname wasn't Sparky for nothing!'

I realized that if I still wanted to be first in this lethargic state, I will need to shine because not living up to my nickname – not me!

Chapter 2
Sparky's Race

At the start of the first day's walk in the terrain to Platbos hut, the forest painted a disturbing picture.

'It was so beautiful last time.' I was utterly taken aback by human greedy handiwork.

'Breathe in Cornelius, just the starting point.' I believed that the mountains would still be incredibly beautiful.

Searching for my backpack amidst the hordes of bags, I notice that girl loading her backpack onto her shoulders.

'My Knysna girl…wait, wait…Knysna-blossom,' I found a proper name for that caring, cute girl. Backpack on my shoulders, I once again stealthily glanced in her direction and realized that I needed to break the ice as soon as possible if I wanted a chance at romance.

"You all know Speedy right?" Mrs. Grobler assembles us.

"Two years ago, Speedy ran the Knysna Forest,

literally…" Everyone burst out laughing at my crazy facial expression I had no clue what she was talking about, but I quickly swallowed my joke as she struck a dead serious look on her face.

"You have already been warned. I won't tolerate it this year. Let nature breathe through you, let its magnificence intoxicate you, drink from nature's water of life, become one with nature…you will not run again!" I became an example.

I was in a situation. How was I to explain to Mrs. Grobler that the adrenaline that drives me to be first every day and the feeling of freedom when the wind blows through my hair completely contradict her beautiful speech?

'I can't, I've to do something.' Such an unknown urgency flashed inside me.

'I can catch up with everyone again later in the day,' I was convinced and ready to take a stand for what I believed. I could not help myself and unwittingly responded.

"But ma'am, I really want to, now, and then let my hair flutter through the wind!"

"Okay Speedy, just you…now and then." I almost avoided everyone's chats, which I felt would spoil my sense of freedom in the beautiful forest.

"Everyone…listen! There are three big rules."

She rolls her eyes as she conveyed the words with meaning, and it completely felt as if I were back in school again. But none the less listened carefully.

"Number one; choose a group and don't fall behind or move out of your group, everyone must know where you are at all times!"

'Yeah…I'm running alone.' I couldn't pay much attention.

"Number two; do not stray from the trails, stay on it so that when you are lost, we can easily find you!"

"And lastly, whatever you do, if you get lost, under no circumstances should you call your parents. They won't be able to help you, and then they will just be worried."

'Yeah, right, me calling my parents?' I laughed inside at her classic joke because I am the best hiker that never gets lost.

"Off you go."

While everyone darted for the long walk, I suddenly realized that the plants needed some water.

'Oh donkey, nature is a bit naughty.' I realized that I intentionally needed to fall behind.

"Thank goodness; I'm a man." I have broken the first rule already.

Looking over my shoulder, I realize that I had already fallen behind tremendously. Without hesitation, I jumped over the bushes, running lightning-fast up the hill, through the long grass onto the road.

Deciding to make up for some lost time, I took a short cut, through the bushes next to the road, higher and higher up the hill.

'Gosh, I'm unfit.' I gasped for air, realizing that I will not be able to keep up this pace.

One by one, I passed by the slow-paced hikers in the bushes next to the path, laughing, until Mrs. Grobler accidentally spots me.

"No! No, no Speedy, didn't I tell you to stay on the track? You can't run through the forest like that. Stay with the group on the road." I was involuntarily forced back on the road with a group.

'They don't enjoy nature.'

I listened to everyone's life, school, and relationship preferences.

'Dang, it is a tragedy.'

I realized if I don't make a plan, I will never arrive at Platbos first. Halfway up the hill, I got a brilliant idea and waited for the perfect moment to execute it.

Unnoticed, I moved up one by one at ease and with speed until everyone in the group was behind me.

I made sure that I was comfortably ahead, and when a turn appeared and no one saw me, I ran like my life depended upon it until I got to the next group.

I would stay with that group under the radar until I got to the front of the group, get comfortably ahead, and then run when no one saw me.

I made sure Mrs. Grobler hadn't noticed me before I joined another group.

Finally, I reached the leading group. It was humorous how they planned everything meticulously. It was evident that I was in the presence of serious jocks.

"For the next fifteen minutes, we will have to move faster because at half…"

'Check that rooster.' I grimaced at the group leader's comic delegation to his subjects.

'You have no idea.' I wormed myself into the middle of the group.

'Only three left…I'm almost out of everyone's noses. One left.' I finally reached the front and suddenly became the new 'rooster.'

My mind filled with fond memories of my previous hike. I was suddenly back in time, carried away to that hike where I slept later and later every day.

I enjoyed the challenge where everyone had about an hour's lead before running through the forest, like a crazy person improving my daily record with greater motivation. One day, I rushed past Mrs. Grobler at a lightning-fast pace, and as a result, my well-earned nickname Speedy was born. The challenge to start last and end first every day was incredible.

Suddenly, a loud noise yanked my attention back to reality.

"Wow, fortunately, did not lose you!"

I quickly pick up my precious water bottle before anyone can pass me.

"Yes, you would rather share your sweets." I remember how unpleasant it was when the water became so scarce, and I had only one empty water bottle.

My grandfather once told me:

"My grandson, you being an adventurer, come and listen to some wisdom." I moved closer with dedication.

"What should you do when you don't have any water?" I thought about the question for a while.

"What should I do if I'm without water? What is the most important thing to do if I am without water?"

I just answered that you should probably go and look for water.

"My son, when you have no water, make sure that you stay away from food. When I was in World War II... I remember it like yesterday..."

My wise grandfather had a way with words and, as always, shared his life lessons in such a colorful way. It was like honey dripping from his mouth, and it was clear that I never wanted to get so thirsty.

"Yes, grandfather, you can live without food for much longer than water."

I realized that without those precious juices; sweets, chocolates, biltong, or salty tuna would be a big no-no.

Very relieved, I quickly took a sip of water and fastened it again.

'Now is the time to put Plan-B into action.'

I accelerated, little by little, faster and faster until I increased the distance between myself and the group as unobtrusively as possible.

'This is my chance.' As the first curve in the road appeared, I ran like a madman with a galloping backpack on my shoulders.

'No one saw me.'

As the road turned straight again and the possibility arose that they would see me, I slowed down to an average pace. The distance between the jocks and myself became bigger and bigger, and I was soon out of the red, almost entirely free.

"Surely they wondered if their eyes weren't deceiving them."

With an injection of freedom, I run around the meandering mountain, and into the distance, without resting once.

"I'm free! Woo-hoo!"

The mountain's echo, nature's sweet noises, the wind's buzz, and my audible palpitations eliminated everyone's noise and carried me through the beautiful scenery with no people around me.

"Only one kilometer left? ...No."

The day was over way too quickly, and with wide eyes, enjoying the last bit of tranquility, I walked around one last turn in the incredibly beautiful forest, up to Platbos hut.

"First! Yippee!" "I told you so!"

A calm nostalgic feeling surrounded me, and as complete peace just filled my heart, I threw my backpack at the door impolitely.

All the colorful memories with my group of 2001, still so fresh in my mind, made me realize how incredibly nostalgic it felt to be back.

"Ah, on that pavement…"

I remember playing music for everyone on my loudspeaker 'contraption' and cooking noodles with a can of tuna on my gas stove.

"Here we talked and made jokes until late in the morning…and there at the hut, I chopped and burned the wet firewood." I was nostalgic.

"I almost forgot."

I quickly headed to the showers but, to my dismay, realize that there is no hot water.

"Oh yeah, now I remember."

Walking through the hut, imagining how everything would play out, I smiled at my choice.

"This bed has the most potential."

I found my bed for the night. I always positioned myself between many beds, where I could be the center of attention.

"I don't want to miss out on all the events tonight."

I rolled out of my sleeping bag, imagining how cozy it would be if my cute 'Knysna-blossom' could be close to me.

"Oh, donkey! I must still chop some wood."

I remembered that I still had to make a monstrous fire. "Everyone should see who the alpha male is."

I nearly finished a whole sachet of *Game* energy drink to give me enough energy for my next challenge.

"Not so wet like last time." I quickly gathered a nice dry pile of wood ready for 'pain'.

"The girls need to know who the strong one is."

I picked up the ax and, with closed eyes, tried to hit a log, but it was a hilarious attempt.

After a few strikes, I managed to get better. I did not want to lose an eye with flying splinters, so I resorted to this clever technique that allowed me to occasionally hit the wood accurately.

Soon I got a whole load of wood ready for my big 'Knysna fire.'

"Only one rule when making a fire." I explained to the splinters and twigs that anxiously awaited to be set alight, that a true alpha man never uses firelighters when he makes a fire.

"Leaves are nature's own wonder firelighters." Soon my 'victory fire' burned, and I also gathered wood for the fireplace. "Fortunately, I did not shower."

Smoke and heat filled the shelter like a thick blanket, and it reminded me of my 'sleep-by-a-big-fire-in-the-field' sessions on the game farm. Probably only half an hour later, the tired pale souls with their colorful purple, red, blue, and orange backpacks made their appearance.

It completely clashed with nature's neutral shades almost visible a mile away.

"Your noise will chase all predators away."

"I've been here for almost three hours…you probably got lost, huh?"

I mocked the very leaders of the groups and was greatly relieved that I could walk alone.

The ragamuffins couldn't believe their eyes when they saw my big fire, and it was evident that they fell for my little white lie.

"Shh, oh, but the w-w-water is…"

It was almost hilarious to look at the shivering creatures with their colorful facial expressions because of the icy showers.

'Maybe tomorrow?' I was content. Before long, my great fire was at the origin of all conversations and a gathering place where everyone could catch up on the day's events and have fun debates about everything.

'Best of both worlds.'

I was so pleased that my plan turned out so perfectly and I was convinced that I missed nothing. My thoughts were suddenly, pleasantly disturbed.

Without control over any of my senses, I instantaneously, unexpectedly, witnessed through the flames of my glowing fire, a breathtaking beautiful figure of a stunning girl.

As my eyes fell victim to sensory overload, I noticed her wet lovely pitch-black hair hanging freely over her face. Open-mouth, I was struck as the heat waves of my fire made her locks occasionally flutter temptingly over her glowing cheeks.

'Oh…you're the gasoline, and I'm the fire.' I glance again.

'Close your mouth Cornelius…she's going to notice you.'

My heart's shudders jerked my mind back into reality, and with a shocking surprise, she sat across from me.

'Oh, you're the…now Cornelius, now, approach her.' I realize that if I don't do something now, the anticipation will devour me.

'Shoo, the fire makes one's hands very sweaty.' I quickly wiped my hands on my jeans.

'Look how she's smiling.'

I leaned back a little just to observe her beauty. I was mesmerized.

Out of her heart, she laughed with her girlfriends about how she slipped and fell. Everything suddenly became quieter and quieter.

'Aww, look how she gestures with her hands as her soft, pretty lips move so fiercely.'

'See how cheerful her big bright blue eyes glitter in the reflection of the flames and…' I realize I am staring again.

'Cornelius, stop it now!'

It's so hard not to look at something so enchanting. It was time to meet her.

What I was about to do is undoubtedly among the top three most stupid things I have ever done. I suddenly got up, completely unprepared for what I was about to say or do.

Without wasting another second, I stood up and marched over to the group of girls like a soldier on a mission. Standing directly in front of the group, I opened with a majestic, all-respecting, all-encompassing "Hi!"

That was it. No other questions, nothing to follow up on, nada. Like a statue, I stood with this huge goofy smile on my face, frozen.

'Murphy should be blamed for this blunder.'

Was it at least an "Oh, I'm so sorry to hear you fell," or anything along those lines.

But nothing could save me from my situation.

In one voice, like a choir, all the girls greeted me kindly and waited for a response, but I stood frozen. After a while, I realized that it was now time to go.

Slowly, my smile turned into a subtle frown.

"Um…okay…I'm going to go now," changed my silence into the pitter-patter sound of footsteps on the way back to the hut. I wanted to kick myself. I was upset and couldn't believe it.

"What just happened?" "When in my life…?"

I decided that it was her beauty that captivated me as I have never experienced it before.

"Just when the moment's not so big, right." I philosophized that you always find the perfect words to say.

Arriving at the house, the fireplace with my wood was burning impressively and I realized that someone had jumped ahead of me.

Without worrying about my debauchery, the whole group moved from the shed to my 'party room,' where we continued to chatter until Mrs. Grobler silenced us from the other room.

"Quiet! You're laughing now, tomorrow is a very long and difficult day. You're all going to need your strength."

We probably whispered for another 15 minutes before a second loud voice crowed with proper authority and convinced everyone that bedtime had now arrived.

Long after everyone was silent, I reflected a bit on the day's captivating events and realized what a great privilege it was to be with my new friends at Platbos hut.

I thought about the twelve-hour days, 30 degrees below freezing [-86 degrees Fahrenheit] fish factory of misery in Scotland and was deeply grateful that I no longer had to endure those suffering conditions anymore.

'What a privilege,' I kept thinking about 'Knysna-blossom' the whole time before a volcanic eruption within, left me fuming with myself.

'What is her name? … Ah, enough time to get to know her.'

I lay peacefully in my sleeping bag, listening to the snoring of a few, uninformed about what a big fatal turn my expedition would take.

25 September

Before sunrise, and without the stirring of a soul in sight, the beautiful song of the birds woke me.

'This is my chance.' I immediately packed everything up to get on the road before everyone else and have a huge advantage.

'I will be there this afternoon!'

My strategy changed from starting last to getting a head start so that I could still enjoy the whole day at Millwood.

'No time for breakfast.'

Convinced that there would be plenty of time to prepare breakfast along the way, I was ready to go long before the whole group woke up.

'Stuck in a group for eight hours, are you absurd?' I secretly filled my water bottle with terrible starch water.

'Today, I want to get lost!'

I was inspired by my great desire to wander a little off the road to a river or something interesting.

'Mrs. Grobler will not mind.' I took a quick photo and with one last 'goodbye' glimpse of Platbos hut I left shortly after seven.

[Platbos hut – The place of much late-night laughter.]

Chapter 3
Sparky Falls in Love

Not far from Platbos hut I noticed a few enormous beautiful trees next to a fork in the road.

I must have been bitten by a big bug when I was younger because ever since I grew up with a tree house on the farm, I have developed a great love for such breath-taking trees and I just couldn't walk past these 'giants' without admiration.

When a big tree makes its appearance, I am always so fascinated to the point where I begin planning which branches I would use to build walls for my tree house.

Suddenly, I got a silly idea. I made an enormous arrow from the branches on the ground to steer everyone in the wrong direction.

"Brilliant!" I admired my beautiful mischievous handiwork, but soon realized that my innocent joke might have harmful consequences.

"Won't be too happy with me, right?"

I decided to write them an encouraging message instead. Good deed for the day done, and with only sixteen kilometers left, I ran like a mad goat.

"Nobody's chasing me!"

I was so overwhelmed by the feeling of being free, that I sometimes ran recklessly around the bends downhill.

"That was so close!"

I laughed and enjoyed how much my mind filled with fond memories of my very first Millwood trip back in 2001.

I remember sleeping in while my classmates got up early to set a record for the day. I woke up very late and started chasing everyone from behind, passing all the groups in record time. I finally turned out of the forest into a wide road about three kilometers before Millwood.

I ran like a madman and broke through the bushes around a wide bend with tremendous strides. Suddenly, I heard the two guys in front screaming like girls and they dove into the bushes for cover.

"Sparky! Just you? Phew, don't scare us like that, man!" The guys almost fainted and were relieved.

"I thought you were a bush pig or an elephant or something." They humorously tried to hide their humiliation, which they failed to do, and I only made further fun of them.

"Don't worry, guys…I won't tell the girls that you scream like girls!" I assured them that I'd keep quiet.

Knowing that every descent has a more significant uphill, I was ready for the incredibly beautiful dense steep uphill. In some places, it is so rugged that those colossal trees and dense forests completely block out the sun's rays. A few kilometers further, I stopped in awe.

"Unbelievable!" I am in the presence of the biggest tree I have ever seen in my life.

I estimate that it would probably be the tallest treehouse-tree in the whole of South Africa, and without seeing the top of the enormous tree I took a picture with my disposable camera.

Ring barked Eucalypts…1876 – 1890.

"So ironic." I laughed at the fact that the only giant tree left had to be an invasive tree. A few miles away, a hidden piece of paradise from the road visibly lead my attention more profoundly and deeper into the forest.

"That's what I live for!" I climbed into the woods with my mischievous smile.

"They are not a factor." I scrambled through the thick bushes and vegetation, over another large chopped tree into the unknown.

"I'm an adventurer!" I climbed like a baboon, on all fours, onto a tree trunk over the water to the middle of the beautiful river where I crouched, totally fascinated by the rust-colored water.

"Our drinking water, right!" I was amazed that such rotten-looking foamy water could taste so sweet and wondered how easy it was to judge others like this rusty water.

"Dang Cornelius, you're too philosophical now." It was clear that too much fresh air was smuggling with my head.

"Where did you disappear without a trace?"

I scrambled back over the plants, dense bushes and trees looking for the path, which suddenly played hide-and-seek.

"Peek-a-boo, peek-a-boo, where are you? ...there are you!"

I couldn't believe that it took me so long to find the path because it was literally in front of my eyes.

"Man, this forest...don't want to get lost."

I was thrilled to be on my way back on the path to victory. Downhill, uphill, from time to time, I grabbed some of the trees around the dangerous bends so that I wouldn't step over the abyss.

"Where do I get my good form from?" I ran slightly disappointed and passed the halfway mark.

"Already? No, man."

Suddenly the appearance of an old mine shaft caught my attention and once again I was forced to have a well-deserved rest.

"Oh, that warning keeps people out?" I laughed at the silly warning that would instead invite people to come in. Well, at least for me, but to keep people out, they'd better say:

"Go on in, waste your time, it's just an empty hole in the mountain." I probably would have investigated anyway.

"Well, this is an adventure!" Excitedly, I threw my backpack off my aching shoulders and searched furiously in my messy backpack for my camera.

Now imagine standing right in front of the pitch black opening of the so-called dangerous mine shaft, ready for action, but guess what? No flashlight. Sparky does come up with a plan.

Armed with my disposable camera, I enter the old shaft. Faced with potential danger, I decided to use my camera's flash to show me the way and blind the potential predators in the old abandoned shaft.

"Okay, just three photos."

I snapped a photo and it gave me a rough idea of what the path ahead looked like. Deciding that I didn't want to waste my film, I moved slightly frantically with shuffling movements, foot by foot into the pitch dark, abandoned mine shaft.

Every now and then I'd give the floor a loud kick, hoping that the noise would warn the who-knows-what inside before I hurt it. The overwhelming damp smell of the mossy soil inside the 'belly' of the shaft became too intense to breathe, and I had to inhale through my old wet, sweaty shirt.

"Six feet inside the ground." I scoffed, because the tense feeling turned out worse than worrying about the hidden surprises inside the shaft.

Without any sight, I slowly walked with my hands touching the damp wall of the pitch-dark shaft, painting an image in my mind of what it might look like inside.

With my eyes more accustomed to the dark, I was amazed at how these miners could dig such a hole with their primitive tools.

My camera's flashes not only blinded my eyes but also contrasted the image of this cave in my mind.

"Always light at the end of a dark tunnel." The way out was much more convenient than the road in.

[Look at the gold ore still in the rock wall. A pity I only noticed it after the development of the photo.]

Outside in the sun with fresh air was wonderful, and I was so relieved that I did not come across a 'surprise.'

After a sweet sip of water and a bite of an energy bar, I was on my way.

After a few 'white feet' *[painted white feet on trees or rocks are signs to show distance or direction]* along the way informed me that the end was approaching. A few meters further, I came across a sign indicating a pleasant waterfall, and I was sold on the idea of taking a well-deserved swim.

"Waterfall means…swimming hole below."

At the turn-off, I headed to the waterfall because I wanted to swim all day long. Through the dense, almost overgrown forest, the ambient sound of the water falling and the cool mist of the water spray reminded me of the icy rainfall of England. I climbed over a tree trunk and through a few branches before standing in the breathtakingly beautiful face of a waterfall.

"Yes, man, extreme."

I wish I could jump off that cliff, but it is just too impossible to climb such a sloping waterfall. As I leaned over the ice-cold water, the time for swimming had arrived, and I needed some motivation.

"Okay, Cornelius." I'm ready to count.

"Five…four…three…two…one." But there I stood in one place.

"Aye, come on, Cornelius."

I encourage myself for a second time, but before I can get too rational, I leaped into the water. As I plunged into the freezing water, it felt like sharp needles prickling my body, and like a cat landing in water, my feet knew just one way – the way out.

[Guess what happened…]

At that very second, trying to get out of the water, I slipped on a big slippery rock, falling chin first on that rock and back into the icy water.

With my chin painfully bleeding, I lay a little longer in the cold water, just to numb the pain. After that refreshing swim, I felt refreshed and not only alive but also incredibly hungry, and decided to cook my well-known two-minute noodles.

"Mm, chicken-flavored noodles with tuna…don't get any better." I realized after that first bite how hungry I am.

After lunch, the dense forest that had surrounded me so tightly before changed into a beautiful valley, and without anyone being able to stop me or steal that wonderful feeling of freedom, I had such a euphoric *'Steve Irwin'* moment and yelled with a loud voice across the valley "Woo-hoo!"

This utter elation and wild ecstasy of being free *[which you can only experience in nature]* has always made me act a little crazy.

"Another white one?"

I am almost disappointed at the realization that I only had a kilometer left for the day because I was easily able to do another five at least.

On the hill before you walk around a bend into Millwood, a sign full of historical information appeared and I was fascinated.

I imagined what it would have been like when gravel roads served as main roads filled with luxury horse-carriages for cars. I wondered what it would have been like when doctors had to decide which toe to amputate due to a horrible nail infection, or when women still wanted to be women and dentists were your biggest nemesis. I wanted to go back in time.

"That life was still so uncomplicated, traditional, and I'm sure the girls..." I laughed around the last turn to Millwood's main road.

"Aah Millwood."

I looked at the tiny town, which dates back to the time when gold fever made everyone sick. The feeling of standing on the same ground in this historic village with its coffee shop, mine shaft, museum and cemetery gave me goosebumps. Without thinking twice, I stepped through the door of the coffee shop with my soaking wet and sweaty body.

"Hello, young man! You're the first chap." A friendly shopkeeper greeted me."

I got nothing out except "Coke, please," because my throat was just too dry and I was desperate for a refreshing soft drink. When your mouth waters for something, it is always the most enjoyable, I thought.

I remember the last time I wanted to have a can of cold drink so badly was after that chili eating contest that did not go down so well.

You see, my very trustworthy friends dared me to eat some hot peppers, and because I have always liked chili, I was sold.

But who would have guessed that Habanero peppers could be so hot? That day there were probably seven kinds of rascals burned out of me, and the Coke that I managed to get hold of with dear life only made it much worse.

In the shop I stared fascinated at a lot of pictures from that period, before I noticed on an old-fashioned clock, that it was already five past twelve.

"Way too long…tomorrow…" I disappointedly decided that on my way to Rondebossie, I would set a record.

[If only I had known that the following day would take such an ominous turn, I probably would have changed my fate somewhat while I still had the chance.]

In the street looking for Millwood hut, I saw some workers quietly enjoying their lunch in the shade of an enormous tree just opposite the turn-off to the cabin.

I greeted the old workers because I had a lot of time on my hands. They were probably the friendliest Afrikaans-speaking forest people I have ever met, and we talked about the bush for nearly a whole hour.

It was so incredible to listen to their interesting tales and stories that happened in this forest.

"Silly animals, these pigs," old Jonas further told me about the dangers of bush pigs and how much damage is done to their vegetable gardens each year.

"…If they chase you, you will have to find a big tree very quickly." Laughs old Jonas that you just see yellow teeth sticking out.

In anticipation, I marveled further at their stories that could not be read in books, before I greeted them kindly and followed the road to the long-awaited Millwood hut to clinch my well-deserved second title.

Arriving at the cabin, as before, I chose the best bed with the most 'possibilities' and made myself at home before taking a piping hot shower for almost a whole hour.

After an incredible shower, I quickly chopped wood and started a fire like I always do. With *Game* energy drink in one hand and an energy bar in the other, I lay cozily in the sun near my fire victorious while time passed by slowly.

"This is living," I smiled.

"My brave knight…can't believe I met you here."

She picked up another grape and innocently put it in my mouth as I looked straight into her beautiful brown eyes.

"A sweet mouth needs honey, my fair lady." She giggled with her modest, brightly lit eyes as I gently prepared her cheek for a kiss.

"Oh, my strong knight."

I leaned over expectantly but suddenly woke up by the crackling of a pan or tin cup on the porch of the house.

"Oh, no." That fairy-tale-like picture was just a stupid daydream.

"Just a very…tasty daydream."

Someone's backpack lay beautifully on the porch, and with a touch of passive aggression, I jumped up and wanted to see who the heck spoilt my fun.

"Did the *Choo tjoe* train hit you? Poor guys." A few guys lay exhausted on the bare beds like tired donkeys.

"Tired…walked very far."

The picture was so comical that I almost felt sorry for them. In a mischievous mood, I told a little white lie that I had been resting on my sleeping bag already since 11 o'clock.

After the guys' reaction I wanted, I smilingly lay in eager anticipation to meet her in my dreams again. But alas, after another half-hour's closed eyes, still did not get me back to my 'Knysna-blossom.' Almost there, but yet again, a loud bang interrupted my desperate search. Just like before, a lot of pale, tired souls and their heavy colorful bags entertained me. Safe out of harm's way in my sleeping bag, I almost pitied the tired, irate, crimson-colored girls.

"So pretty…but yet, so rough."

I smirked at those who just could not care less about the aesthetic value of the forest.

"Oh, just stay out of their way until the hot water is gone." I got the desired response from the girls on their way to the showers.

Almost like watching a nature movie, the picture of an uncontrolled herd of wildebeest escaping for their lives fills my mind, and I realize that that bathroom is really in danger.

'Thank goodness I am done.' With way too much energy left in the tank, I jumped up and decided to go and explore Millwood.

Walking into Millwood, I decided that the cemetery on the left will be my first destination because I have always found graves incredibly fascinating.

"Knysna-girl?" I suddenly remember that after so many hours, she has not returned yet, and I started chasing ghosts.

'What if she got lost?' Concerns plagued my mind.

"If she is in trouble, then it will be my duty to save her." "I can be her hero." The whole picture of how it might play out blew my mind, while excitement sparkled. "Dude, you could be her hero!"

I moved with the biggest broadest smile, faster and faster towards the cemetery because I firmly believed it to be a shortcut to Millwood's main road. At the cemetery, I suddenly stopped jogging and walked dead civilized with all due respect until I was through to the other side before I ran full steam again.

"Still enough respect for the dead." I smiled.

"Ah, was a shortcut... my direction in nature is brilliant."

I jogged back over the hill with my intuition which had never let me down.

Past that historical sign, where my thoughts digressed a bit, back down the hill, across the open plains, where I shouted 'woohoo' in elation. Suddenly I heard approaching voices, almost demoralizing.

"Oh no, man, she must be missing."

I realized that my chance of being her hero might be ruined if I cannot save her. In the direction of the noise that sounded like girls approaching, I ran with my head turned to the side so I can hear better.

"Don't be her!"

"What are they laughing about?"

The nearly familiar sound of her voice, almost ironically confirms that it is her. But I kept running like a dog about to lose its juicy bone in the direction of 'danger,' again without a clue of what I will say when I see her.

At that unexpected moment, she made her appearance, my eyes met hers, and as her beautiful wet, pitch-black sweaty hair fluttered over her face, Cupid shot me with an arrow in the heinie and my legs just completely went numb.

It is a miracle that I remained upright because, at that very moment when she appeared without warning, I staggered forward as if I sprained my ankle.

It must have seemed pretty comical when my right knee almost hit the ground without falling. I suddenly jumped up and stood in front of them again.

"I just slipped…over some stones."

I tried to camouflage my red-glowing cheeks with my head upside down, laughing together while searching for some stones on the ground, but could not find even one.

"Where are you going so fast?" I heard her asking a question in the most beautiful sugary voice.

"She…spoke to me…?" Shock and surprise hit me at the same time.

"Look at her beautiful smile…her soft, bright, light brown eyes. Look at how fiercely her beautiful pretty soft lips move and, if you look there…flip it, beautiful is just beautiful!" I got beguilingly excited.

"Hey big fella, where are you running so fast?" She does it again.

"Run?" I suddenly wake up from my trance. "Me…?"

"Yes, I do that thing…" I laughed a little embarrassed as she looked a bit confused by my response.

"Um, probably just because I wanted to…" I hesitate for a second.

"…You see, this forest is so beautiful, I just can't get enough of it." I recovered just in time.

She wanted to say something else, but I decided that I needed to jog before I am caught off guard again.

I wanted to offer to carry her bag because she looked like she was going to fall, but I could not because just offering to carry hers would have given me away.

"Jeez, I had fun talking to you girls, but I still have to run to the gorge before tonight…so, see you at the hut." We all left.

'Jeez…I still have to run…' How pathetic.

I must have kept running for a whole kilometer before I finally stopped and turned back to the direction of the cemetery. Just too many indescribable strange feelings plagued me and I could not decide whether I was happy, semi-embarrassed, or frustrated with myself or the situation.

"Of course, she wouldn't get lost, Cornelius. She stayed on the road, stupid!" I was finally upset and ran as fast as I could just to cool off a little bit.

Back at the graveyard, I realized something disturbing. 'So many graves of children?'

I wondered if an epidemic or something happened.

'Life was not easy at all.' It was clear that their struggle for survival was surely a day to a day race.

"Enough of the graves."

I ran back on the winding gravel road, over a hill, around another descending turn, until I found an old-fashioned locomotive parked under a roof.

"So that's what the trains looked like at that time... probably transported gold ore?"

It was incredibly interesting to see the caves and ditches where they mined, back in the day. Some of the poor miners even used their bare hands to mine.

While walking back, reflecting on their hardships, I had the utmost respect.

Back at the hut, my heart skipped a beat, because I could not believe the happiness that fell upon me. On the lawn, right in front of me, I came across that beautiful 'Knysna-girl' without any of her girlfriends, acclimatizing all alone on her blanket in the sun. I was excited like a boy in a candy store, because '*Bambi*' was separated from her herd.

'Oh, that light pastel-pink color top.' She was just perfect. I scraped every bit of courage together to approach her because she was just way too beautiful. Breathing in, breathing out, I took action before I got wet feet.

"Hey...been so long since I spoke to you..." "Did you survive the hectic hike?"

I tried to melt some of the broken ice with my infamous 'Calvin Klein-goofy-smile.'

"Oh, hey blondie...yes, well...at least."

She was so cute with her genuine friendly laugh. She told me how much that backpack hurt her poor shoulders and that there was no hot water left at all.

I moved slightly closer and knelt on her blanket. Before long, we conversed as if we have known each other for years, and I had to stop myself just before I fell deeply for her.

'No other place in the world…' I lay beside her, very proud, looking deep into her eyes. It was breath-taking how her eyes glittered as we whispered sweet nothings.

I only wanted to touch her hand once, but fearing that I would spoil the perfect moment, I waited a little longer.

Like gunshots, my heart began to fire, and afraid that she would hear it, I remembered that I did not know her name yet. Suddenly I got a smooth idea and put on a serious face.

"Golly, can you get it over your heart to forgive me for being so impolite?" I tried my best not to laugh as she looked at me, surprised.

"You know I've been talking to you for so long…" She nodded.

"…I haven't even bothered to ask for your name yet." I smiled teasingly.

"Oh, silly, you."

She slapped me gently on my hand and laughed so adorable.

"Then I'm also loutish…my name is Nicky," she blushed.

"Enchanté mademoiselle, my name is Cornelius…or you can call me Sparky."

We shook hands, and as our hands touched, we gently almost instinctively looked into each other's eyes. Her tender laugh did not exactly hide her blushing cheeks.

By the time the first star made its appearance, I was surfing on cloud nine. This was truly an indescribable moment, probably a thousand times better than perfect.

As *'a whole new world'* extinguished all sounds and words in my mind, we soared. Between her and me, time stood still.

In a sudden moment of weakness, I almost said to her:

"My sweet red lily, I ran, especially just to see if you were okay." Fortunately, I did not. Maybe I should have?

Without saying a word, and with our hearts beating audibly, we slowly began to study each other.

Her eyes, that beauty spot on her cheek, and nose, on the spur of the moment, I accidentally touched her hand. At the same time, our eyes slowly studied each other's lips.

My breathing became heavier and heavier, and without control over my knees, started bouncing rhythmically to the beat of my heart. Suddenly, I quickly stole a breath of air before suffocating. In slow motion, we swiftly moved closer and closer to one another while closing our eyes at the same time.

'Cornelius, now!'

'Now, before the moment's gone!'

A millimeter before our lips touch, just that fraction of a second between happiness and *Murphy,* am I completely pulled back to reality by the worst horrible crunchy voice.

"Oh, here you are hiding…searched the whole world for you."

I am upset that she spoiled my perfect moment with her imperfect timing.

"You have to see the cemetery Nicky." I swallowed my disappointment while my anger was still running a little wild.

"Oh, wait…did I bother you?"

She asks so graciously, while literally in my mind, I see the friendly picture of a wild boar ramming her from the side.

"You are so considerate! No man…you didn't bother!" I recovered with a smile through my teeth.

"Nicky, we moved to another room because we don't want to sleep with them in the same room…get your things, we're moving."

That girl's tone sounded just too commanding! I just had to stop myself from showing the 'reed rat' how badly she started to work me up.

'What…Nicky will sleep in my room if she doesn't move?' I realized that I should do something quickly to stop that 'cave-otter's' plan.

"You won't believe me, but that room has a nice fireplace and it's Millwood's 'party room.'

"We will have the best evening." I do not know if my subtext persuaded Nicky to stay, but I tried my best.

"She doesn't want your so-called 'party room.' She will sleep in our room. Thank you!"

"Come, Nicky!" She is given no choice, and I am almost a wild boar.

"Why should such cute girls always have such… girlfriends?"

I quickly helped her fold her blanket. With her blanket in her arms, and her eyes locked onto mine, we almost had the last moment without saying a single word. We just knew.

As if her friend really had her knife out, she totally destroyed our moment again while glaring defiantly at me.

"I almost forgot Nicky, Robert called. Better call him back. You don't want to lose your chance of love."

She greeted me kindly with warm, heartfelt eyes and a tender, gentle smile as she turned and walked away.

"Beautiful, just beautiful!"

I stayed a while longer to pick up the shards of my 'Knysna dream' in disenchantment and let it all sink in.

Finally, with a tear in my smile, I returned to the fire, convinced that as beautiful as that 'Knysna-girl' is from the outside, she shone much brighter from within.

The pleasant chatter and jokes at the campfire about a distance away, had me torn between two worlds.

"Where was I all day? ...Oh yeah..."

The beautiful, piping-hot fire with its bright red, blue, and white glowing coals occasionally ignited my rhetorical thoughts before I let some of my discontentment out in silence. I did not want to think about that lost perfect moment. But before anyone could say knife, I was again crowned as the heart of the party.

As a positive character, I always have a way to rise above any difficult situation. I once again entertained everyone as usual with my jokes, daily dilemmas, and anecdotes for which Sparky is well known.

Later, the group moved to the 'party room' in front of the fireplace, before a friendly warning to consider everyone, allowed the hungry sounds of the fire to soothe our thoughts symphonically.

On my bed, wrapped in my sleeping bag, I once again lay awake listening to U2's *with or without you,* and pondered at the day's events. In my heart, I wished I could have listened to this beautiful song with her.

Because this beauty of the forest that we experience in all its splendor is so overwhelming, one can just fall in love with the idea of being in love.

Long after everyone was asleep, I just lay there and watched how quietly my 'Knysna-princess' slept like an angel.

'She decided to stay! She stayed…'

It suddenly dawned on me. I sighed nostalgically before my disappointment yelled inside. Drained by my mundane ride of euphoria and disappointment, I continued to watch the flickering of her shadow against the wall with empty thoughts and emotions.

Chapter 4
Sparky Gets Lost

I awoke drenched in sweat from an awful nightmare. Frightened, confused, and cold. I touched my shoulders and then my heart that did not want to calm down.

"Wow, luckily, just a dream Cornelius, just a pretty bad dream."

I tried to convince myself and took out my phone to see the time.

"Oh no, I forgot to put my phone on charge again."

I switched off my phone to conserve that last stripe of battery life that was left.

26 September

It is dew before dawn and the flickering image of my 'Knysna girl' along with the calm, soothing sounds of the fire served as a lullaby. As this almost too realistic dream sent icy shockwaves through my system, I notice that the once large, blazing fire with its flickering silhouette on the wall is now reduced to a pile of coal and ash – just like my hope.

'If only I can see her image again.' I suddenly jumped up and threw another log on the coals.

'If only she…come, Cornelius, the sun is sipping water.' I interrupted my trail of thought and started packing my luggage as fast as possible. Around the door, I was surprised to see that the log was on fire, but before I could see a final glimpse of her silhouette, I forced myself through the door.

'Lot's wife turned into a pillar of salt' I snuck foot-by-foot across the creaking floor so that no one would wake up. In vain.

"And where are you going so early?" I suddenly froze in my tracks as the unexpected sounds of authority glared at me.

'Darn it, I've been caught.' A proper delayed reaction rippled through my system.

"Mrs. Grobler! …uh…afternoon, evening…morning, ma'am." I tried not to look too surprised.

"…Oh, I…I am searching for some water for the long haul." My head left me for a little while.

"No…not water…ma'am…I seek advice for the long haul, yes." I recovered almost convincingly with a naughty smile.

"Advice for the long road? What advice Speedy?"

"Advice…uh…advice for the long haul?" I scrambled ferociously in my mind to escape from that pit I just dug.

"Ma'am, I am afraid to get lost here in the forest." "Yes…I am afraid of getting lost."

I made the most innocent joke that I could think of at that moment because I knew that there was a higher chance of finding a 'KFC' in the forest before I would get lost or even ask for directions. My white lie quickly saved me from the situation none the less.

Suddenly, Mrs. Grobler's face froze up with a 'smack-me-with-a-wet-fish' expression on her face.

It was obvious that it made no sense for Speedy, the speedster, the 'Knysna King,' to be afraid of getting lost, but she sympathetically still continued to give me direction.

With half an ear, I listened attentively as she explained the way.

"When you pass the cottages on your left, you will come to a fork in the road where you have to make sure…" I already lost track of what she explained so thoroughly.

Every now and then, I shook my head without having a clue what she said.

"Yes…" I nod in anticipation that she would finish explaining because as a right-brain dominant creative person who lives for purely the aesthetic aspects of our world, I never could absorb too much information.

"But Speedy…aren't you going to walk with the group shortly?" She did not even finish her explaining.

"Ma'am, I would rather run alone…give my mind some wings." I camouflaged the truth after yesterday's blunder, hurriedly.

"Besides, I can't walk so slow, but thanks anyway, ma'am." With my water bottle filled, I am ready for the day's adventures. Almost out of the door, in a playful mood, I pulled Mrs. Grobler's leg.

"Oh yeah ma'am, let's just say…hypothetically, so that I know…what should I do if I'm really lost?"

I laughed when her ominous look explained so courteously what would happen.

Millwood hut just behind me, I quickly snapped a photo and through the lens of my camera reminisced for a second how beautiful the moment was that I shared with my Knysna girl.

"There we were…" The camera's clicking noise gracefully interrupted my thoughts, and without looking back, I headed on the path of no return.

[In retrospect, I do not believe that I would have made that innocent joke if I knew what was waiting for me, but how was I to know that that harmless joke would turn out so satirical.]

Despite the fresh, breezy cold morning, I started my adventure with flowery surf trunks. I suddenly remembered Fraserburgh *[pronounced Fraserburre in Scottish, go on ... practice that Scottish accent]*, a small icy fishing village in Scotland. With the very same surf trunks that a Canadian gave me as a gift I caused quite a buzz in the little town.

[One cold winter morning, I was fed up with conformity and decided that I am going to be a proper South African. In the middle of winter, I bravely walked through the streets of Woolacombe, a little English town with only my sandals and swimming trunks. People started taking pictures of this mad fella. In the end, a photo of me appeared in the local newspaper with the caption: 'summer spirit.']

"Past the cottages and then left, or something…?"

I followed Mrs. Grobler's careful instructions in my mind past every beacon but hit a little snag when I came across a 3-way fork in the road.

"What did she say again…?"

Faced with three choices as the road split left, middle and right, and a no-access sign directly next to the sign that indicates the way to go, I am absolutely disoriented.

"Which way should I take?" I try to figure out which path seems most correct through the small dilemma.

"Three roads; a no-access sign and only one 'white-foot' next to the no-access sign?" I am indecisive.

I remembered one of my favorite poems *the road not taken,* and just like Robert Frost, I am standing in front of a big forked path in my adventure, which may have an unknown and potentially fatal outcome.

"The group may not overtake me."

I anxiously chose the big wide path on my left.

"If I get lost, I will like before find my way back again." I trusted my perfect direction outdoors due to my previous experience, growing up on a farm.

I strolled like a protagonist in some 'Greek tragedy' downhill on the path to tragedy, stage irony at its best. A short distance later a small path forked into the broad road I traveled on, and I was convinced that the road with the no-entry sign turned into mine. But oblivious to what was going on, I carried on walking in the wrong direction for probably another half an hour without noticing a single 'foot' sign.

[On any hiking trail, the white feet indicate direction and distance. One painted foot simply shows that you still

must move forward in the direction that you were going and that you are on the right path. If two feet are painted side by side, horizontally or vertically, it means that for your good, it is best to turn to the direction in which the feet show.]

"Boy, did that gravel road fool me?"

It felt a little like I had taken the wrong direction, but not too concerned, I carried on walking for a while until I realized I really did.

"So, I got it wrong."

I try to find a solution to my little problem, but there weren't any. As in a chess game where you must choose which one of your precious pieces to give up in a lose-lose situation, I am faced with a choice with terrible repercussions. If I turn back, I will have to be satisfied with being last, or if I take the adventure path that has not yet been trodden, I will definitely get lost like a buffoon. As a result, like Robert Frost, I took the road not taken.

"Do at least something every day that scares you, because if life doesn't scare you, then you haven't lived…" I stay true to one of my unwritten rules.

Arriving at the 'T-junction,' I follow my instinct which has never let me down.

"Rondebossie…mmm…right."

With my intuition which I believe can challenge the ladies, I carried on.

Over and over, through the mountain, I was totally captivated by the beauty of the forest, and just like Hansel and Gretel grabbed hold of the 'sweets' and got deeper and deeper into trouble with the horrible 'witch.' I was driven by my urge to the unknown, deeper and deeper into tragedy's hands.

"H…y…dro?"

I approach a sign around a corner a long distance away from me, only slightly visible with squinted eyes.

"Oh, hydro."

A beautiful white 'foot' suddenly appears that indicates the road to a Hydro on my left, and I am slightly annoyed.

"Just beautiful, you're only missing for like three hours."

A wide good-natured smile appeared on my face.

"Rondebossie must be on your right; don't worry, Cornelius." I did not let the smell of doubt turn into a concern.

"Another fork in the road?" My intuition was tested again after about three hundred meters uphill.

"Straight on or further up on the right? Right."

My solid direction convinced me that Rondebossie should be to the right.

At the top of the hill, I reward my tired legs by rubbing the cramps out of my calves.

"Today might take a little longer after all Cornelius."

I realized that I might be a little lost when after about four hours of searching did not produce the road I was looking for.

Up the mountain, a gulp of water, around and down the mountain, another sip of water, and once again over the mountain. It was clear that I am not making any progress.

As another downhill presented itself, I ran like a wild stallion driven by sparks of euphoria down the winding path until my sense of freedom suddenly turns into utter disbelief. *"Murphy!"*

Severe disappointment rippled through my system, almost comparable to a middle child dropping the only scoop of delicious ice cream on the floor that was left over by his two brothers. Suddenly my mood sank right into my shoes.

"Dead-end? …Dead-end!"

A deadly concoction of shock, disappointment, and anguish hit me. The road not taken led to a mountain in front of me that hinted at the end of the road. With only one sane option; to turn back.

"Cornelius, can I tell you a secret…" I whisper softly in a calm voice followed by a thunderous:

"I think…you are…lost!" I roared in anger at my situation.

[This was my last opportunity to turn back to safety, unharmed, unscathed but without pride. Unfortunately, I did not accept the invisible no-entry warning sign.]

"I did not walk so darn far for nothing!"

Up and down I searched for alternative options, rather than what obvious logic presented. After careful analysis, I slowly walked to the edge of the precipice.

[My famous last words…]

"Does not look so bad? "

Determined and dangerously-stubborn, I carefully climbed over the edge, but before I could secure my grip, I slipped and lost my balance. I slid for about two meters, before tumbling head over heels forward and, as a result, fell knee-first, through a large broken log. Agony, pure agony.

"Uh, Ou-ch, flipping hell-oh!" It sounded as if someone stood with their full weight on my stomach.

I was in intense pain while blood gushed out of my knee. I lay in the mud and compost-like leaves for a while longer just to get used to the discomfort.

Out of the mud, I looked at the distance I tumbled down from and was quite impressed.

"That is one for the books!" I see to my astonishment, everywhere I look, broken branches and fallen trees are scattered, almost like when Simba ended up at the elephant graveyard while on his expedition.

"Elephants are having fun with these trees."

I realize I will have to watch out if I do not want to be trampled on. Nature's bright sounds and splendor, blended with my indescribable feeling of freedom, caused a sudden euphoric reaction.

"Woo-hoo, the adventure of a lifetime!" I suddenly realize that I am treading where no other has been before. I am making my own tracks in the forest.

"Now you are exploring, Cornelius!"

"No set route; every step is a step on my way. Mine, you explorer!" I carried on perilously deeper into the unknown.

"Thank you Lord that I have the privilege of walking here in your beautiful forest. I am so happy. Thank you, very much dear Lord, amen."

Over the muddy, very slippery steep downhill, I slide with great difficulty due to my hurting knee, trying to keep my balance. It literally felt as if I am trying to walk on a slippery ice-skating rink with flip-flops, and it was nearly an impossible task. As I climbed over the crisp, wet, mossy tree stumps like a baboon on all fours to a meandering river below, I happily donated life to my empty water bottles.

"Wow, first time for the day." I was relieved by that stream of grace.

"A lot scarcer than last time."

I filled my water bottles to the brim, and as my stomach growled, I realized that I had not eaten in ages.

"When was the last time I had any food?"

It was time for a breather and I gladly threw my backpack to the floor. I quickly enjoyed a piece of biltong *[dried meat/ similar to beef jerky, but way better]* because there was no time for cooking.

Suddenly, complete enigma struck. I fiercely searched through my backpack and threw everything out while disbelief kicked in.

"One can of tuna? How the heck is it possible…"

"Last night, when I was cooking? No, what am I going to do?" I smiled when I realized in my haste this morning while it was still dark, I forgot all my supplies.

"Yes, Cornelius, your 'survival test' is now more challenging." I bundled everything from the ground back into my backpack.

"That is why you pack everything the night before!"

I was perplexed about how I would survive but decided to be thankful for that one can of tuna and the packet of noodles that did not end up in the bag next to my bed.

Right in front of me at the bottom of a vast steep rocky mountain, scattered with dry, dense branches and shrubs, I stand before nature's 'burglar bars.'

"Come and try…you won't!"

It seems like that first obstacle of the day provokes me.

With my backpack on my shoulders, I try to determine in vain if there might not be a shortcut past or around all the mess. Slightly knee-deep, I stand alone against a crowd of 'guards' armed with spears, almost like a Ragged-tooth shark ready to defend their kingdom.

I must get through to the other side, so I took my first step to the foot of the mountain and suddenly got scratched by a branch.

"*Eina*! You have to watch where you walk!" Irritated by the branch, I kick it a few times to show it how it hurt me.

"Nice, hey!" Another branch and yet another one gets my wrath before I am deeply scratched again. I tear through another.

It is almost as if a pattern develops while the branches still remain too dense to penetrate at all.

"It's war!" I turn the negative situation into positive energy as I hide my half-filled water bottle and wipe the sweat from my forehead.

In my imagination, I transformed my circumstances into a game where I had to fight like a Cavalier alone against an army of soldiers. Every time I was scratched or cut, a little of my strength was sapped, and when I broke a branch one of their soldiers was dead and I was one step closer to victory. The displacement of reality in the form of a game slightly camouflaged the reality of my situation. It was fun and games until the overly frustratingly painful 'got me's!' versus my aggressive challenging 'got you's!' received the best of me.

Through the overbearing frustratingly tiring challenges, my sanity was slightly affected and I wanted to find a way out of my problem quickly.

"Yes, brilliant idea!" Convinced, I started counting back from ten until I had enough courage to break through the branches at full speed – with intent, force, and determination like a medieval battling ram.

I made it through the first one, almost through another branch, until the unbearable blows to my ribs, interfered with my fortitude, became physically too much to bear.

"Go Cornelius, go!" I try to convince myself that a little blood is not the worst, but as the burning cuts and wounds on my arms, legs, face, and stomach intensify, I'm forced to stop. As I am catching my breath in pain, I realize how stupid that was.

My blood sugar has suddenly dropped sharply, and while I am quivering, I struggle to get my water bottle out.

"Oh no! Can't be true?" I realize that nature has intruded. I look in complete disbelief at my empty water bottle.

"Probably when I stormed through?"

"I have two water bottles, only two! For the whole walk, and now you're empty!" I vent in frustration.

"Oh, Lord! Please help me through this.
I need your help, amen."

I reached a low point with my water supply and realized that the luxury of drinking water was no longer possible.

I drank the last few warm drops that remained in my empty water bottle. I have to keep going, but find myself stuck in the middle of a legion of thorny sticks standing side by side like armed soldiers. The excessive heat, thousands of sharp 'spears', the doubt whether I am still on the right path, and the fact that I was not going to reach Rondebossie first anymore, started to get to me.

"I have so many scratch marks." I decided, despondently, sweaty and exhausted, that a few more scratch marks would no longer make a difference.

Ready for operation 'break-through-the-branches-number-two.' I shut my eyes and clenched my teeth before counting down.

"Ten…three…five…seven." I stormed ahead, knowing beforehand that this will be a foolish choice, but it was too late.

"Crack!" I am suddenly stopped dead in my tracks by a thick branch.

Determined, I continued as I always dragged those tires during Rugby practice at school. As my momentum slows and numbing pain starts to intensify, it confirms that my attempt was by no means successful.

With my wind knocked out and a tear suddenly forming, I struggle to gasp for a little air and I am not able to even sit down on my haunches.

"Oh, flip, that was stupid!" I rest with my head against my knees, wishing that I could only lie on my back for a little while, but in this position, it is impossible.

"Look at my bleeding legs."

It was clear that each thorny branch had to be broken down separately if I wanted to get to the other side.

As I gently pull myself up against a thorny branch with the sleeves of my jacket over my hands for protection, I suddenly feel a severe stabbing pain in my ribs.

"Ou-ch! It hurts!" I realize that there is something wrong with my ribs because simply breathing requires more effort.

Through the maze of thorns, I carefully break down one of those branches, which surrounds me like an ambush. Another scratch mark, another wound.

Occasionally, my backpack clings to the abundant thorny branches, yanking my body painfully.

"Yes! Want to hurt me, you worthless thorns!" I started breaking the branches instead of just removing the necessary thorns in my way.

Eventually, through the thorny maze, I screamed with joy because it felt like a millstone fell off my shoulders.

"I'm through, I'm through!" I grabbed my last filled water bottle and gulped.

My dad once told me when we climbed Blue Point at Montagu, Western Cape, that it is better to take slow sips of water until your body has cooled down, otherwise you just sweat precious fluid, but beyond thirsty, it was impossible to only take small sips.

"Wow, it's so much better." The sweat flowed across my forehead, and I felt slightly guilty about my water supply, I stowed my water bottle emotionless.

"I'm ready to tackle you." I looked at the big steep hill and realized that the only way I will overcome this Everest is by setting healthy, positive goals. Trees that provide shade and trees next to big rocks became beacons.

On all fours, I grabbed tree branches, bushes, stones, and anything that could help to overcome the steep ascent. Past beacon one, I rewarded my hard work with positive thinking.

"Almost Cornelius, almost at the top…you're going to make it. Above, you will be able to look out over the valley…you will see where to go!"

I do everything in my power to stay positive.

*"Dear Lord, when I am at the top, please let me see the
way. Help me find the right direction, please, Lord,
amen."*

"Just a few meters more Cornelius, there lies the crest…almost at the top."

I finally reach the top of the crest with severe disappointment. It felt like nature was playing tricks with my mind.

"Why is the slope of the mountain the same? Are the trees and bushes still so dense? Nature is not sparse at all!"

I am by no means blessed with a view over the valley, and it is nothing like I imagined.

"Am I at the top or not?" I am confounded.

"It must be the crest!" I stand on the top, but I can only still see about five meters in front of me due to the density of the forest.

"I should have been able to look over the mountain by now." The one thing I trusted to give me hope and motivation did not become a reality, and I struggled to keep that same positivity.

*"Dear Lord, please show me the right way. Lead me on
the right path, I implore You, Lord, amen."*

It was clear that my nerves were wearing thin because my faith in myself to find the way, diminished quite substantially. I break through a few more bushes, and, in front of me, there appears a small hidden old deserted path.

"You were made by an old tractor!" My hopes lit up positively.

"Thank You, Lord, thank you so much, amen."

Right there and then, I turned left on the deserted path to see if it could lead to water because I was in desperate need.

"This road must have been used years ago." Several trees about two meters high grew undisturbed in the middle of the road in peace. It was clear that Mother Nature took back what belonged to her.

"I will arrive at Rondebossie in a while." I walk with new courage and a broad smile, knowing that my excellent direction has not entirely failed me.

Suddenly, a branch scratches my face, and that intense pain quickly pulled me back to reality.

"Nothing will discourage my new courage!"

I process my pain in silence, followed by a pleasantly happy skip in my step because, for a change, I do not have to endure an uphill battle against the sun. Back in the aesthetic beauty of my mind, another thorny branch sinks into my arm.

Still, with my newfound sense of calm, I yanked my arm out of the thorns rather than wasting a moment to pull it off.

"You won't scratch me again!" I get the idea of not being bullied by nature so severely.

"Tracksuit pants are out of the question." I pull off my tracksuit top and hang it like a screen in front of my legs while I fight down the high cliff against the thorny branches.

"Another split in the road." I laughed utterly clueless.

"Do I have to go right up the mountain, or rather down the dense cliffs?" I experience another Robert Frost moment.

"Road is too dense." I turn right up the hill but quickly realize my mistake.

Before long, the path gets so bad that I have to climb over branches and later use imaginary tractor tracks to see a road.

The slight signs of a road, later turn into an imaginary path and are just too dense to know where I am going.

"Burned unnecessary energy!" I scramble back over the branches and bushes to where I take my last sip of water with blank emotions.

"Need water urgently." I block out the realization that I am in trouble before it weighs me down any further.

"What am I going to do? Water doesn't flow so high." No easy way off this mountain, I am in deep trouble.

"I'll get water!" I move blindly parallel to the cliff along the high precipice on the dense path ahead, rather than risking my life with the cliff.

"I won't climb that cliff again." The path twists before I have to climb a steep uphill again.

"You see, Cornelius, you're over the dog's tail. Almost at the hut." I get hopeful when, about two kilometers away on the other side of the incredible precipice, a broad gravel road with huts appears on the other side.

"Must be Rondebossie?"

"With no path to get there at all!" I feel a little frustrated again.

Every step through the bushes, I am reminded by a constant little voice in my head that my route would require unshakable perseverance, courage, faith, and help from above.

"Don't despair, Cornelius, just be courageous!" I carried on slightly frustrated with burning groins on my way to 'who-knows-where.'

[The whole 'rash' test reminded me of when I was about ten years old. I went to the Rustenburg fair with jeans and bought many interesting but unnecessary things. Because I did not have a backpack, I kept stuffing my pockets until I could barely walk. At the end of the evening, the result, no doubt, persuaded me that it was a huge mistake.]

"Winners don't quit." I walked with discomfort through the bushes and tall grass to where an incredibly beautiful enormous tree almost on the edge of the abyss convinced me to take a break first.

I decided that the beautiful tree with that large rock under its branches was my well-deserved resting place.

"Wish I could sit like that all day and forget about everything." I escaped the scorching sun's raging rays under the shade of that remarkable tree.

Dear Lord, help me to not lose hope. Help me find the right path. Lord, please get me out of here, show me the way, if it is your will. Please, dear Lord, amen."

This was the first time my reality became a reality as cracks started appearing in my positive state of mind. With closed eyes and oxymoronic thoughts flashing like a television without a signal, my body suddenly filled with an unfamiliar feeling.

[Now this premonition is hard to explain to someone who has never had this experience. I will not blame those who believe that I am merely twisting truths, because I even started thinking that nature was playing mind games again. But how does one explain such a phenomenon?]

"There's something behind me!"

Suddenly my eyes open wide in a staccato reaction. At the same time I am covered from head to toe in goosebumps, followed by a nasty shiver that persuades me that I am not alone.

"Ba-boom, ba-boom, ba-boom, lub-dub…ba bump!"

I slowly turn around – when you expect the worst and waste just enough time to get your nerves under control, before facing the inevitable.

Suddenly I realize with one big shock, "I am not alone!"

Seated on the rock, I suddenly see a short round plump man standing with his about fourteen-year-old son under his arm, looking straight at me.

"Surely miners from the eighteen hundreds?" I tried to make sense of it all. Dressed in khaki clothes, broad-band hat on the head, pickax over one shoulder, and a spade in the boy's hand, rounded off with the friendliest broadest smiles on their faces.

The funny thing is that I was not scared at all and as a result, I reacted a bit flabbergasted and responded to their gestures with a continuous thumbs up. I completely believed that their kindness was I sign that I would make it.

"The miners brought good news." I experience a new sense of hope and courageously believed that I would safely maneuver my way out of the clutches of the forest.

"This is a-ma-zing!"

I could not care less if my positivity was the result of temporary insanity because I found new hope again.

"The miners from back in the day also walked here, and they survived." I was so excited about my adventure of a lifetime that turned out better than my wildest imagination.

"If I arrive at 20:00 tonight…those girls will be a little worried, awesome!"

I analyze how I will catch everyone off guard because everyone knows that I am the fastest runner.

"Let everyone worry a little innocently, sympathetic factor with the girls, perfect!"

I laugh at my waterproof plan, which has come to light so unexpectedly.

"Awesome." I believed in no other outcome than getting safely to my destination while caught up in the aesthetic beauty of my thoughts.

"Dé-jà-freaking-vu!" I laughed when the road a few hundred meters down met another dead-end.

Without being discouraged at all, I turned straight to the steep slope without worry.

With my thoughts as good company, the soft and muddy moist soil reminded me of that incredible snowboarding expedition at Mount Hut, New Zealand, where I bravely skated down a very steep slope on all fours.

The refreshing cool air under those prominent 'skyscrapers' and large ferns kept those murderous sun rays away, but with no river in sight, I became very thirsty.

"Almost-almost." I confidently believed that water should not be too far downhill over the tree stumps. "Whoa." I accidentally tread through a massive moss-covered tree, probably five times my width.

"Dang, that's crazy." I am stunned that this tiny 'toon' was able to break that large tree stump, and out of sheer pleasure jump on another tree.

"Dang, that's cool." My face suddenly brightens, and, like a blast of energy, I almost carelessly jog down the slippery slope. "There's a stream! There's a stream!" But I was fooled by a mirage on the horizon.

"No, how is that possible?" I frantically moved up and down, looking for signs of life because I just could not accept that the stream had dried up.

"Why have I wasted water so many times?" I remember how I always washed that darn car with a garden hose. I carried on searching without stopping.

"So, thirsty!" I wipe hardened, white sticky sweat off my lips.

"How many disappointments?" I raged with nature after my initial joy turned into utter discontentment.

With my back against the wall, I removed a few damp leaves on top of a ditch, and to my relief, dripped a few drops of brown water. It looked exactly like an old rusty leaking tap that dripped now and then. I cannot think of another time in my life when I was so relieved to see hope-giving water.

Before, I would not have touched it, but without a choice, I was just so grateful.

Because that drip-drip seemed so tearfully close to drying up, without delay, out of breath, almost hurriedly leaned face first over the drops.

To my regret the pungent, damp, dead, musty, mucky plant stench hit me like a fist in my lungs. "Ugh!" I immediately yanked my neck away, almost spraining it in the process. Again, I bend over carefully, holding my breath, exhaling through my nose because I learned my lesson.

While shivering, I sip that dull brown, greenish moss-filled, wonder juice drop by drop until I gasped for air again. Repeat.

"Grace!" I sat soaked with a full stomach in peace, thinking how many people have to deal with this problem.

"Nobody cares man. Later it is news about sports again." I realize how guilty I am. With my bottles full, I am again courageously ready to tackle the ascent in high spirits.

"You're a monkey." I realize how senseless I was and then developed a 'happy' skip in my steps toward the foot of another mountain. I had a lot of reasons to smile again.

A few bushes, trees, and twigs further up, this sweet familiar noise positively interrupted my favorite songs in falsetto.

"Yes." I realized what this rushing noise high up on the cliffs signified, and it left me almost emotional because of the distance problem.

Suddenly, I felt like a little boy at a candy store without any money, embarrassed, as a sturdy ice-cold stream unexpectedly made its appearance.

"Where…the…freak were you, huh?" I think a little reluctantly, back to that rotten water I just drank a few minutes ago. I just shook my head and refilled my water bottles with this icy 'miracle juice' because it just smelt, looked, and tasted sweeter.

[Now there is an unwritten rule in the forest when it comes to a descent. I call it the calm before the storm because every 'friendly' downhill has a steep 'unfriendly' incline. You will see what I mean.]

"Tranquility before the storm." I smile in the face of a monster, but grateful to have found a new life in my survival game.

Those nasty thorns did not contaminate this part of the forest, but it was covered by a combination of beautiful yellow-greenish thorny covered flower-leafy-plants.

[Now those plants reminded me of an ice-cold syrupy sweet-toothed-lip-laced sweet-toffee apple that you had been craving all day, but because your mom spoke you waited until after dinner. After you cleaned your room and vacuumed the carpets [my mother is not really so strict], you excitedly, hastily sink your teeth into that ice-cold syrupy mouth-watering-sweet toffee apple, as deep as you can that a piece just sticks to your palate.

Then you realize to your great dismay the juicy worm that also came to visit is slightly uninvited. There are things in the forest that are aesthetic and looks so beautiful, but underneath it all can be dangerous.]

With zest, passion, and courage, I take my first step through the beautiful green-yellow blanket of thorny beauty.

"Dang, you've got a bite." I smiled because in nature, you are always faced with new unique challenges.

Everywhere around me, under a dense blanket, the mountain was covered with thousands of razor 'teeth,' probably a meter or deeper. I was completely fooled by their 'shiny top, smelly bottom' motto.

Foot by foot, up until my arms through the dense yellow-greenish razor plants, again reminded me how foolishly I bruised my ribs without cause.

"I underestimated you, right." I relentlessly tried to pave my way through this endless blanket of frustration with painful scratches and mind-numbing knocks on my extremely sore ribs.

As a result, I amusingly watched how blood flowed elegantly over my already-skinned legs.

[I remembered movies of how people armed with machetes broke through dense jungles.]

"Wish I had a *Panga*-knife, I would have shown you!" I dragged my heavier-than-usual legs.

[The hidden yellow-green thorny plants behind the trees.]

"No, this engine doesn't want to work anymore." My legs got stuck yet again, and without hesitation I ripped my legs out of the clutches of those thorny plants.

"The group is probably already at the cottages with ice-cold juices, cookies, sweets, and chocolate, relaxed next to a fire I should have started." Destructive negative images filled my mind.

'They are not thinking about you.'

'I cannot take it anymore. I'm so tired!'

"No, block it out Cornelius, almost at the top." The positive angel just kicked the cynical devil in the face off my other shoulder.

"How long ago did I eat?" My growling stomach reminded me yet again of my circumstances.

"Mm…tonight I'm going to have a wonderful dinner…my delicious can of tuna." I licked my dry lips.

[On the menu tonight…let's see…my last can of tuna a la King, fresh off Spar's shelves, on top of a bed of incredible lip-smacking delicious steak-flavored pasta imported from Italy. Get yours today for only two rand thirty-nine, yes ladies and gentlemen you heard right before last year's inflation rate.

But wait…there is more, you not only get the beautiful packaging with your pasta for free but massive discounts as well. Can you believe it? Take your time but not too long. Yes viewers, with us, the buyer is usually right, so we will only ask you two rand thirty-five.

Incredible right…a full four-cent discount that you can do with whatever you want. Can you believe it? I can't.

Yes, ladies and gentlemen, we don't just look out for your pocket, but don't care about your trivial little things. I laugh at my unique attempt at television salesman.]

"Oh no, you're so bored." I realize that when you are slightly taken out of your comfort zone and allow the unwanted sounds of your mind free reign, you start doing the strangest things.

"Today is a good cardio workout." Sweat flows again over my face.

"Hardly any carbohydrates, a lot of sweat, a lot of hours, if I keep going like this I'm going to get my six-pack soon." It feels like I have probably burned twenty thousand calories.

Almost up the hill, the steepness begins to flatten out, and again it filled me with little flashes of courage.

"See Cornelius, almost over the dog's tail."

I do everything in my power to keep going forward but as before, I realize that nature has interjected.

My thoughts freeze in silence while my heart pounds.

"Go find your water bottle." I wanted to forget about the world for a second while I process my shock, without wasting a second I threw my backpack off my shoulders.

It was like I was a puppet on a string, trapped in a Chinese melodrama with nature being the puppet master.

On my way back through the dense razor plants without the heavy backpack, the positive relief in my crooked shoulders causes me to walk off balance.

"There you are, my lost bunny." I spot my water bottle with great relief. As I haunch down to pick up my red water bottle my eyes are given a chance to see what goes on underneath it all, and suddenly a frightening more sinister truth is revealed to me.

"Oh, shh, not cute!" I grab my bottle in terror, knowing that I could be a victim, at any time. Just to realize it is nearly empty.

"Dear Jesus, I didn't want to know.
Please protect me, Lord, amen."

I have never been arachnophobic, but knowing that in this dense forest thousands of colorful eight-legged 'brothers and sisters' were all around me, my comfort zone threshold relentlessly shifted again.

"Get out, get out!" As quickly as possible, I rush to where I threw off my backpack. I did not want to fall prey.

"Faster! If they can sit, they can bite." I propel my backpack forward so they won't have a chance to sit or bite.

"There are more! Please, do not bite!" I realize that I am in grave danger.

"Dear Jesus, please help me.
Don't let them bite me, amen."

I carried on rushing painfully up the steep hill blocking out any thoughts of spiders.

"Calm down Cornelius, calm down, you're hurting yourself." Once again, the path I created became more gracious downhill as the 'razors' and its spiders become sparser.

"Give me a snake rather than a spider." I reason down a steep downhill that snakes are more predictable and at least easier to spot.

"Everything looks toxic!" I shiver again at the thought that those nasty black-legged red and orange spiders crawled all over me.

"Violin-spiders, Button-spiders… *[South Africa's most poisonous spiders]* …what do they look like?"

Again, I climb without fear on top of a big old fallen tree, suspended halfway over a cliff in the air.

"My kingdom is beautiful!" I sit with my legs hanging over the stump in mid-air and then suddenly get a bright idea.

"Maybe, I have a signal?" I am tempted to switch my phone on, but because Mrs. Grobler's rule number three plays like a 'gramophone record' in my mind, I am slightly indecisive.

"I'll just check the time." I am convinced I won't break her golden rule.

"Don't die, please." The late afternoon sun shines directly in my eyes and onto the screen.

"Don't call your parents if you get lost...don't call..." The glare on my screen is way too intense, and I have to turn it a few times before I can finally see.

"15:40...Do I have a signal? ...I have a signal!"

"*Thank you dear Jesus*, sorry Mrs. Grobler." I wait in suspense for someone to answer.

"Please answer..." One dash of battery power. "Pick up...pick up!" My anxiety becomes deadly.

"Hello Dad, thank goodness! ...Yes...it's going well...Dad, I need help! I am in a lot of trouble! What should I do? What should I do?" I ramble like a salesman all in one sentence.

"I'm calm...I don't know where I am...I am lost!"
"Talk faster, please! My battery is going to..."
"...Hello...hello!" My phone died.

I switch the phone on again and frantically dial the numbers.

"Don't die...hello...yes...the phone cut out...I'm on a cliff, high on a tree stump...the sun is right in front of me...on the other side of the cliff...where should I walk?"

"Follow the river to the sea?"

"But…it's too far, it's impossible…Hello? …Hello? Darn it!" My phone cut out one last time and I was overwhelmed by severe frustration.

"Laugh at your ass, man!" I respond to the mountain's fun poking echo as I hang-glide struggle-struggle from the tree stump to the very steep gorge holding onto those razor plants to neutralize the mountain's steep descent.

[Like a scrap of hidden grace, these 'creepers' actually came to my rescue because without those pestilences, I would never have been able to get off that height.]

Faced with a descent at an angle of almost ninety degrees and without the luxury of touching the mountain beneath my feet, I must abseil using the creepers to regulate my momentum down the mountain.

"Absolutely breathtaking." Every step I take it is as if I am walking on a blanket in the sky without touching the mountain once.

For a moment I forgot about the spiders, because I had never walked on a 'cloud' before.

"Freaking awesome!" I was so grateful to have made progress from the high mountain, and as each timid step down the slope turned into elaborate strides, I started gathering too much momentum.

Without caution I accidentally hit a 'bald' spot on the mountain and my momentum increased instantly. It was like going down the 'Slide of courage' at the Valley of waves literally falling for a fraction of a second. I suddenly fall over that rocky mountain two, three, four meters before my backpack graciously gets stuck in the yellow-greenish razor creepers with significantly less skin.

"That was just wrong!" I roar at the mountain relieved as my pounding heartbeat begins to calm down.

"It was…close."

I waited for a second longer, processing some of the frights I endured the last hour before venturing down the steep slant again. Time was running out fast.

"Every minute wasted is one minute less of healthy daylight." I have to get out of this highly dangerous area as soon as possible.

"Dear Jesus, help me. Lord, do not take away the daylight. Just a little longer, save me, Lord, please keep me! If it is your will, Lord, amen."

As if the whole day's jumble of destructive 'activities' weren't enough, there was a more significant cunning danger waiting for me. In my mind, again, as before, a flashback of previous experiences has secured new courage.

[A few years ago, I decided to walk along the beautiful golden beach of Struisbaai [Struis bay], – the southernmost point of Africa to where my eyes could reach, because it was one of those personal challenges of mine. After being almost bitten by a seal on the beach, I swam through a river and got away from aggressive seagulls that constantly attacked me. After a whole day I eventually arrived at Arniston. That day I was reminded of how the Lord provides in His wonderful way. I was dead tired and plagued by

inflammation in my feet after probably walking on sand with flip-flops for about forty kilometers [±25miles].

After my only bottle of water, the ten-rands [$1] worth of biltong, and three bananas were finished, I physically did not have any strength left to go on any longer.

I was exhausted, hungry, and dehydrated. Just when I wanted to give up there was something special for me, a gift from above, a brand-new bottle of Energade miraculously on the beach. That allowed me to return to the resort with enough energy.)

"I'll make it again, the Lord will provide." I ignorantly moved closer and closer directly to danger.

[I have been catching snakes for years and ever since I was a little boy the danger has always fascinated me, but when you almost, unexpectedly, step on an aggressive snake, you can't help getting a fright.]

"Three…two…one…"
Suddenly I get an adrenaline overload as my body instinctively reacts in overdrive.

Instantly jumping backward grabbing those creepers, and suspending myself with supernatural strength as if I had never had an injury before. This sudden aggressive hissing noise convinced me that what I just stepped on was deadly!

"Oh, no!" My heartbeat ripped through my chest as I tugged my shaking knees under my chin, waiting for danger to pass.

Like a monkey on a branch, about a meter away from the enraged snake I clung for life until the bright, colorful snake slithered away.

"It was too close, too close!" My body still shivering while letting out a big sigh of relief.

At the moment the snake struck, instead of hitting my leg, it bit into a twig less than two inches in front of my leg and missed.

"How? …how? …how is it even possible?" I was astounded.

"Thank you dear Jesus, thank you so much for your miraculous protection, amen."

[Flashbacks of my naughty days as a child on the farm reminded me of those incredibly superfast scared housemaids as I chased them with live non-venomous snakes that I caught on the farm.]

"Shame, they were so scared." The terror I experienced felt almost justified. I let out a sigh of relief again.

"I have to get down from these 'clouds,' I won't be able to stay here longer."

The minutes under my feet increased positively, but 'healthy' daylight decreased at an alarming rate.

"Dusk is probably an hour away?" The clamor of falling water near the approaching cliff begins to awaken euphoria inside me.

[It was a sign of hope, an injection of optimism that I might still find my way back before dark. I was optimistic

that I would get off this treacherous mountain – alive! I could almost feel the sweet taste of grace over my dry, cracked lips.

But what I did not realize was that this next test presented to me would become my biggest struggle for survival to date.]

"Almost there, Cornelius." I was encouraged as the gentle soothing spray of falling water got closer and closer, stronger and stronger.

[Without warning within the infallible sounds of hope, a cold, darker, sinister truth was about to be revealed. This type of truth should preferably be avoided as far as possible, but when comforting snippets of past experiences becomes the result of an inevitable heap of anxiety. Then there is only one simple question that you must ask yourself: How badly do I really want to survive?]

Closer to the edge of a dangerously high cliff that unexpectedly appeared in the twilight, I climbed through the increasingly sparse branches and 'creepers.'

I was introduced to its unfriendly brother with its triangular razor-sharp 'blades' for leaves.

"Night is fast approaching."

Distracted, without conceptualization of rational thoughts, in an unexpected moment, I absent-mindedly climbed struggling over the cliff with a bundle of 'creepers' in my hand to a soft, unstable, damp patch of earth about six feet below. STUCK!

"Oh, no! ...oh no! ...oh, no! What did I do, Lord...? What did I do...? I wanted to come down so badly...but I didn't look, Lord..."

A shock wave of anxiety and disbelief rippled through me when it dawned that my small judgment error might be the last of me.

"Why didn't you look? Why did not you look, Cornelius?"

Reproachful questions of anguish played over and over in my mind where I am stuck between heaven and earth.

"I am just too weak. The hurt is just too much for me to pull myself back up so high."

It was overwhelming! It was majestic, incomprehensible leaning over the terribly high precipice due to my backpack pushing me forward.

"I don't want to... I..." Turns my disbelief to realization, and is it almost impossible to utter my thoughts.

"What should I do...? What should I do...?
...Oh, dear Lord!"

Suddenly my panic-stricken screaming for help, broke my trail of thought because that ruler-wide patch of moist soil could no longer carry my weight.

Between me and what was probably an eighty-foot fall to my death, the patch of earth beneath my feet slowly began to sink like quicksand.

Desperately, I searched for an alternative ending.

"There..." Because my life depended on it, I climbed with trembling legs onto a thin tree trunk that grew next to the patch of earth on the side of the mountain wall. Having no other choice, I hung over the precipice, with only one small tree carrying my weight miraculously.

"Don't die now, Cornelius!" I clung to that tree of grace anxiously. I realized with concern in my heart that I would never be found if I were to fall and was by no means ready to enter eternity.

"Surely this is it, Lord? I do not want to. I cannot, not now! I still have so much to accomplish in my life, Lord. I have yet to meet my dream girl, and I am only nineteen."

The fight against my sanity and the onslaught on my mood just become too heavy to bear.

"I have so much pain, Lord, I can't take it any longer, I have no more strength, and I am so thirsty..."

It is already dusk and this severe monotonous anxiety has long passed my handling point.

"How much more, dear Jesus? Help me, I cannot die now. I'm losing my mind, please, Jesus, help me...Help me!"

[Trapped in the belly of my cold reality, between life and death, in a fraction of unprecedented silence, soothing flashes of my life and precious moments played out like a movie.

The almost comforting snippets that reminded me of how much I have to lose suddenly sent my will to survive into first gear.]

"Don't wait for better days." Immediately I move up the steep trunk, with my hands painfully-secured to the overhanging mix of razor-sharp cutting-palms.

Stepping higher and higher up the dangerously curved branch, while adjusting my grip to carry my painfully worn-out body toe-by-toe closer to safety.

"Only one slip…goodbye Cornelius." The razor blades of those palms cut even deeper more painfully into my tense hands as I move higher up the slanted tree trunk carefully, foot-by-foot.

This was like a nightmare from which I could not wake up, and my greatest fear became reality. "Crack…" My pounding heartbeat alarmed a thousand panic-stricken words to my heavy breathing and shaking body as an unexpected crack sent the graceful tree eighty feet down to its 'death.'

Instantly, everything turned hazy as my "Á-á-h" screaming disturbed the serene sounds of the 'dusk-beetles' and tranquil nature as I agonizingly fatigued, hung gracefully over the cliff for dear life.

Because of a heavy backpack along with gravity, the 'blades' of those nasty 'cutting palms' sliced deeper and deeper into my hands.

Blood started dripping from my hands onto my forehead and into my eyes, along with the 'tense' drops of sweat flowing to my cheeks like tears. Through the onslaught of my injuries, arm-by-arm, with superhuman strength, I lifted myself back to safety without ceasing.

Back on the cliff, dry droplets of emotion and unbearable pain, vengeful shaking hands and shoulders swore at me.

"Look at what you look like. So sorry!" Emotions overflowed as I gently rubbed my raw hands on my shirt without comfort.

At least I was safe, back where I started, still next to death and aware of approaching darkness.

"If it wasn't for that 'cut-palms'…" I lower my head in silence.

"Thank you so much, dear Jesus, amen."

I almost get emotional again after a painful flashback of my close escape, reminding me of how terribly close it was.

Sands were running out of my hourglass as dusk was upon me.

"I have to get down … how?" Cautiously, I approach the edge of the dangerous precipice, searching for a chink in my fate's armor. The eighty feet must have turned into probably sixty-five by now.

This was clearly my last possible relatively safe option off the cliff before the path would reach a dead-end a few feet away at the dangerous waterfall cliff.

Because my choices off the cliff could not become more favorable at all, I once again sailed with palms, plants, and tree roots in hand, gliding-sliding over the cliff and down the slope. Step-by-step, I gradually move sideways in the direction of the waterfall until the heavy backpack and steep precipice below almost made me fall off the cliff again. Stuck!

"DéJa vù!" Once again, I anchor my sandals in the damp earth and urgently examine my surroundings for more favorable options. About ten feet down, perhaps three feet from the waterfall, I notice a tree.

"No, Cornelius, you're going to die." I look in fear at my only route to grace and I am not at all convinced. For a moment, I close my eyes.

"Please, please, just carry my weight!" I find myself in a dilemma.

If I jump over the cliff and miss the branch, I will fall to my death…and if I am so lucky as to catch it, there is the other possibility that the branch could break due to the humid air and years of damp waterfall drops.

"I'm going to make it! I'll make it!" This just gives me enough motivation to fight off my overwhelming fear.

"Please, don't break!" All my injuries flashed like warnings in my mind of how bitter it was going to be.

"I probably need to get down." I anxiously plead with the tree one last time, and without losing another grain of sand from my precious hourglass, a simple "three… two… one…" helps me over the slope.

[As if I am stuck in a time warp, making surrealistic decisions just to stay alive, my inevitable choice for survival spoke volumes when that ominous cracking noise persuaded me that I caught it.]

"Got you…don't break, please!" Shock waves drive my sobering emotions of anguish, like a constant seesaw ride, and as I try to curb every droplet of sentiment against the loss of courage, I slowly bow my head in agonizing pain.

It was incredibly disappointing to realize that it was my shoulder instead of the branch that was so cacophonic superior.

[Similar to watching a movie and from the very first moments your senses get bombarded negatively, my chapped-chafed arm served as an introduction to a nasty nightmare concealed under my shirt. I did not want to move, I could not breathe, and I didn't want to let go. I was too scared to analyze my injuries because my sanity was nearing the 'abyss.']

I realize that there is no other tree close by as a connection to get down the dangerous slope, and without any other way out, I have to turn to the waterfall. With nowhere to hide from my crisis and fast-approaching darkness, I just clung to that branch with shut eyes trying to forget most of my pain.

"Oh, dear Jesus, just take the hurt from me.
I no longer know how much my body can handle anymore,
amen."

Again, I muster up the courage and with no other outcome, I slide down the moss-covered tree trunk with most of my weight placed on my legs until only an arm's length stands between me and the dangerous waterfall.

"So here you are." The entity I most wanted to avoid winking at me.

"No other way out." I look at a possible outcome in distress, privileged that I have not succumbed yet.

"You're not going to give up now, either." I prepare for my most dangerous stunt.

With my weight fully resting on my legs, deflecting as much pain as possible from my sore shoulder, I test the credibility of a few dry rocks next to the waterfall.

To my disapproval, I realize that the rocky 'waterfall-road' is not safe at all. Without effort, chunks of the rock break like clay, and I am gripped by fear again.

"Onslaught upon onslaught." I break the rest of the fragile rocks until it feels strong enough to possibly support my weight.

Suddenly my eyes catch a 'taster' where the rocks hit that rocky bank about fourteen meters down. "Don't look down, Cornelius! Have you not learned anything from the movies?"

My breathing quickens while my legs cannot stop shaking as if they know, "get away from here before it's too late." Death was ready for round two.

"I don't want to fall!" I pull out a plastic shopping bag and put my most valuable possessions inside, like my disposable camera, CD-Walkman, matches and my pocket knife, to protect it from the waterfall.

After I securely fastened the bag to my belt, I turned my gaze to the majestic waterfall.

"Ladies and gentlemen, this is what you have been waiting for, our grand finale … Sparky the Daredevil, the 'Knysna King', is going to show you the stunt of a lifetime. Exhausted and dehydrated from the day's setbacks, plagued by raw bleeding hands, injured ribs and a possible cracked collarbone, he will attempt to descend the dangerous, unpredictable waterfall without a rope some fourteen meters to his death… uh… safety."

The ridiculous image of a big fat circus announcer hyping the crowd, fills my imagination until I have just enough motivation to go against all warnings for their enjoyment.

Armed with a final shooting prayer, I am ready to test death in a fifty-fifty situation like Russian roulette.

"I suppose I'm ready?" All friendly logic fades, and with full concentration, silent, audible breathing, and hands on the rocks, I leap from the tree to the waterfall with a final flick in my legs. A sudden, painful twinge in my shoulders shoots through my body, and with violent blasts of air from my lungs through my mouth, I instinctively try to numb the stiff blue pain.

"I didn't fall! ...rock carried my weight?" Cautiously amazed, I am still 'safe' in the air.

But with each passing second my joyful vertigo diminished bit by bit.

My backpack, the nasty knot in my muscles, sore ribs, injured shoulder, and wounded hands, started to become the end of me. I was seconds away from falling.

I could not hold on any longer because every movement of my legs, shoulder, and hand in unison downward was followed by a nasty jerking bounce by my backpack.

I was left with no other choice than to get rid of my backpack. With one arm still anchored to the rock I quickly hooked my other arm out of my backpack strap, and with a quick exchange dropped my backpack from my shoulders to the rocks below.

The loud thud my backpack made on the rocky riverbed below sent alarming caution-filled warnings.

"I'm so sorry!" I used every bit of effort to forget about the unbearable pain and kept climbing down the wet slippery rocks.

"Hold on…just a little longer!" I keep fighting against nature's onslaught.

"You're not going to die, Cornelius, you're almost there!"

My urge for survival became more urgent, and with each gasp for breath, while clenching my teeth, I climbed above my physical strength, further down the waterfall.

The distance below became less, but I was too heavy for my injuries. With the pain too unbearable, I was facing certain death.

"Hold on, Cornelius!" My less injured shoulder started to weaken due to the continuous overcompensation for the injured one.

"I can't! …I can't…I can't anymore!" But carried on, while drops of dangerous relief started to loosen my grip.

"Hold on Cor-ne-lius!" I shouted at the top of my lungs so I would not let go because I really did not want to fall.

"I don't want to die, I don't want to die!"

"Hold on!" My grip is slipping and while trying everything in my power to adjust my wounded hands over the rocks, I am face to face with death.

Without warning, the waterfall-cliff made a deep opening, and having no foothold, my feet suddenly dangled down dangerously into the depths. Everything went weak, and when my arms gave way under the overwhelming strain, enough was finally enough. Without any time to recover, I approached death backwards with my last plea in anticipation:

I do not know how long nature was blessed with deathly silence, but as everything began to sink in, the silence slowly turned into a loud symphony of noisy cheers where the cliffs could laugh for a change at themselves.

"Dear Lord, I made it! I'm alive, I'm alive…I made it thank you, thank you, thank you, dear Lord, amen."

Completely overwhelmed with joy, I realized that I experienced another humongous miracle. I landed right on top of my backpack safely with my upper torso, back, and head – like a pillow – without sustaining life-threatening injuries.

[I'm sure that even if I won the Lotto, I wouldn't even have been so relieved, because I had overcome the biggest challenge of my life with grace from above.]

"Probably eighteen, nineteen?" I try to work out how high I fell. I was flooded with intense relief after realizing how blessed I was that my arms did not give in earlier. With my feet back on the flat rocky riverbed, I kept staring at the steep cliff for a while, knowing that I should have died. I could not fathom how I managed to fall right on top of the backpack.

"Oh, thank you, thank you, thank you for breaking my fall." I embraced my backpack, which lay halfway on the stone riverbed and shallow water.

"You're a little tattered…just like me, huh." I nodded in admiration.

"So sorry, man, but I would have died." I explain carefully to my backpack that I did not have any other choice than to let it fall so high. Amusingly I noticed most of my two-minute noodles in the river.

"Mm, dinner." I laughed because it was slightly longer than two minutes in the water. I could not care less because I was given another chance at life.

"You don't climb off a cliff like that again, Cornelius." I felt confident that the worst was over while I gathered most of my sunken noodles in my pot for later use.

[The worst was happily over…or was it?]

"Where will I sleep tonight?" With my backpack strapped back onto my incredibly aching body, I struggled through the middle of the dry Knysna River, looking for the best spot away from the 'nightmare' cliff where I could rest for the night. I struggled laboriously over the washed out branches, trees and boulders. It was obvious how the previously flowing river had ravaged everything in its path.

"Dang, you were mad, weren't you?" I stared without despair, hungry, sweaty, happy, hurt, safe, and in good spirit at the first major challenge that awaited me after the horrific cliff.

"This is where I'll be camping tonight."

I looked with a broad smile, uncomfortable at a very different type of challenge that blessed me with its presence.

I realized that if I wanted to protect myself at all from the cold and deadly dangers which include caracal, leopard, and other wild predators in the woods, I would have to look for firewood urgently.

"Mossy, damp, or rotten."

My grandmother's wise words played out in my head when that futile search only delivered a tiny pile of miserably damp wood.

"That's why you don't work in the dark." I smiled.

[It was inevitable that this fire-making excursion would be quite challenging, because it is impossible to make a fire with wet wood, right? Wrong.]

Armed with a can of Shield deodorant in one hand and matches in the other, I produced a blow torch flame like a Bunsen burner and burned the living madness out of the damp wood until it caught fire.

After my delicious last tin of tuna with those washed-away beef-flavored noodles, I lay in my sleeping bag next to the cold fire and listened in silence to the variety of night sounds that darkness brought about. It was unreal and allowed me to forget about all my problems.

The golden, dancing flames almost in sepia, produced sweet, nostalgically soothing, flickering shadows on the rocks and I remembered how cozy my 'Knysna-girl' slept that night.

"Wonder what she's doing now? …What is everyone doing now?" I smile shyly at my rhetorical questions.

"Hope they don't have a party?" I wonder slightly meddlesome who that guy was that contacted her.

"Who knows, maybe she is a little worried about me being lost in the heart of the deep, dark, dangerous Knysna forest?" I smile a little controlled before the ominous sound of a breaking branch nearby grabbed my attention.

"What was that? ...ugh, probably a leopard again?" I mockingly brush it off while the previous rustle in the grass was replaced with an authoritative noise of a few moving stones probably fifteen meters away from me.

"Oh, what, out of my control." The symphonic rumbling of the rippling water across the river pebbles, literally a meter away from me, was so relaxing.

With the flames as conversation, I listened to nature's orchestra while wondering about the next day.

A concoction of mixed feelings stirred inside my soul because of all the unanswerable questions I was faced with.

"How am I going to get over that obstacle?" "Will I ever get out of Knysna's claws?"

"Will I have the privilege of ever seeing my family and friends...? *Mielies* my doggie... and my sweet 'Knysna-blossom?" I could not help feeling a little nostalgic.

"Next time, my mother may listen to her favorite radio station in the car for hours on end."

"...Next time, I won't hit my brother again...I probably shouldn't have struck him when he broke my CDs?"

Without a place where I belong, I lay with my head on a rock afflicted with all kinds of self-reproach.

The presence of an aggressive baboon occasionally roared his voice over the cliffs. It made me wonder whether he wanted to warn his tribe against some kind of forest danger, he either loved the flattering sound of his voice or just maybe tried to agree with my guilt.

I no longer wanted to play 'hide-and-seek' with that insoluble solution to my crisis and just escaped to the splendor of the night. I smiled at that silly tree-hugging-myth that could not take my loneliness away earlier in the day. Quietly and securely wrapped in my 'cocoon', I glimpsed one last time at my obstacle.

"Aye...tomorrow's problem." The moonlight shone through the thick treetops like sunbeams, yielding compassionate rays of hope for the next day. As I calmly listened to the serene lonely sounds of my cold 'hungry' fire, I found peace within.

I was no longer a slave to fear.

[My Shield deodorant spray can, rucksack, flowery trunks from Canada, and the rocky surface where I slept that night.]

Chapter 5
Sparky Makes a Plan

"The black plastic bag, the black plastic bag…" I woke up with a bright imaginary flashing light bulb on top of my head that might just work.

27 September

It is a cool refreshing Saturday morning, and with my cold fire that only turned into a sign of grace, I realize that I survived. I wiped a few condensed sweat droplets of anxiety from my forehead, with great relief.

"Yeah man, I freaking survived!" I gladly rejoice with those hordes of early morning birds and insects at the top of my lungs. I was in total elation because the threats of the night did not come to fetch me in my sleep.

"Shh, last night was rough." As I struggle to sit upright in the dusk of the new day, I am ready to face my battles head-on.

"You white river stones were pretty rock hard hey." I smiled slightly, trying to straighten my extremely tight spastic back.

"Ouch…will get you." I grabbed one of those big stones that I slept on and threw it at the mountain as hard as I could. In my mind again, nasty flashbacks of the previous day's rollercoaster ride bombarded my emotions painfully, and I grabbed another one.

"Nice hey…take that you monkey!"

The loud thud against the mountain persuades me to grab another, and another, until my good shoulder is too sore to carry on with my silly game.

"That will teach you to rouse me from sleep like that." I rubbed my tired shoulder.

[Stuck between two steep, high rock walls, I look out at the dark, icy river dead end, probably as long as an Olympic

swimming pool. If I want to make it out of my epic adventure in one piece, I've no choice but to swim to the other side.]

"Swim or sink … sink or swim." I make a simple rhyme to my crazy black bag idea.

"This black bag idea is either going to be incredibly stupid or incredibly brilliant!" I explain passionately to the thousands of birds and insects listening intently.

"Tweet-tweet, tweet-tweet-tweet, chirp-chirp." They agreed.

"Desperate moments lead to desperate decisions." I force my oversized backpack into the plastic bag my mother gave me for my dirty laundry just before I got in the car on the way to the bus.

"On your marks…" The ominous dark water reminds me of a close encounter with a crocodile I had at Vaalkop Dam in the Northwest Province a few years ago, and I pause for a moment before trying again.

"Wait, wait, wait…what if there's something in the water?" My imagination swam away with me, but after a while I compose myself and look at the water with defiant eyes.

"Okay Cornelius…" I'm ready to sing this icy tune, for the sun would clearly not be breaking through these cliffs anytime soon, miraculously warming the water.

I clasped my hands tightly over the opening of the black bag as I climbed into the water with peculiar "Phew, phew, phew…" sounds.

"Sh-oh, but the w-w-water is cold." I slid across the slippery, loose rock, holding on with my healthier shoulder. I didn't want to slip and fall, but when the rock broke my trust, my backpack and I plunged into the freezing water without mercy. Driven by adrenaline, I kicked as my head touched the water as if my life depended on it, sending my sandals flying in all directions. *[It was all over, goodbye Mrs. Grobler! Tsamaya sentle ditsala yami…or was it?]*

Suddenly my eyes widened in amazement as the black bag miraculously transformed my backpack into a life buoy, mercifully buoying me up as long as it did not get any water.

"Awesome!" I could hardly believe that my plan was actually working, but I pedaled on, for I was only halfway through the eerily dark, icy water.

Out of breath, I continue to fight against the water while protecting the opening of my 'floating device' with my good shoulder as best as possible so that my backpack would not sink before reaching the end.

"*A*lmost there, almost there…" I swim knees first full steam into a large rock.

"Darn, I didn't see you at all." I try to rise unsuccessfully from the now, shallow water but am caught off guard by another sharp rock. "Ouch!" I bite my teeth as blood flows carelessly from my aching shin.

"You just don't want to leave me alone." Back on the riverbed I take my backpack out of the black bag, very irritated.

"My plan worked, not completely dry, but not at the bottom either." I wait in anticipation for my flip-flops while they float, with all the time in the world, peacefully to me. All on one leg and then on the other, I try to dry my body with rhythmic movements.

I realize with my exotic colorful shades of pink, red, light blue, and a touch of purple in some places how I had turned into a chameleon with all these attacks.

"Gosh…I need to get a medal." I once again leave my bag behind and investigate.

"Sparky, the explorer." I climb over large rocks, washed-out trees, branches, and plants where I try to tread.

"Wow, you were angry hey." I marvel at the spectacle of destruction that a proud river caused.

"Am I ever going to get out of here again?" My mind is once again under attack by the overwhelming flashes of the previous day's traumatic events.

"Oh, come on Cornelius, pull yourself together!"

I fight back against my doubtful self before ending up in unfavorable company again.

It was not even three hundred feet further before stumbling block number two arrived for the day, and I had to fetch my bag again. While walking back I created a silly song.

"Over trees, shrubs, rocks, dodging bees and thorny trees, spikey branches, creepy monkeys, rocky edges, funky stenches, scary trenches, not to mention through the river, will not quiver…Over trees, shrubs, rocks…" Again and again.

I sing and laugh repeatedly at a silly rhyme that helped me forget about the monotony of going over all the obstacles again.

"Here you are, shame, my broken backpack." I pick up my neglected backpack and scramble with my "Over trees…" rhyme back to stumbling block number two.

"It's a number two!" I laughed when I realize that I must swim yet again because the second river was a lot worse than the first one.

"Oh man, I am almost dry." I once again enter the freezing waters with my backpack secure inside the plastic bag, reluctantly. Not yet halfway inside the second obstacle, fortune once again swings in nature's favor. My backpack suddenly gets heavier and heavier, holding me back, dragging me down, and sinking deeper and deeper.

"Swim Cornelius, swim!" It becomes a battle trying to get my backpack to the other side, swimming with a tattered shoulder, before sinking.

"My fall right now…probably punched holes in the black bag?" My instinctive urge for survival fuels me against giving up.

"I'm so exhausted! …I've never been the best swimmer." I am caught up in an inner-conflicting, anxiety-ridden survival journey against time.

"Probably an entire Olympic pool length left…swim Cornelius!" My backpack is almost too heavy to hold up with only one arm.

"You won't drop me now…" I fight with my backpack forward before it hits rock bottom.

"Almost there Cornelius, almost there!" I kept dragging my backpack beyond my endurance until my knee slammed straight into a rock, slowing my cunning effort.

"Ouch…made it!" I breathe out two thoughts at the same time.

Dragging my backpack under the water behind me was extremely tiring. I could not help losing my balance over the slippery rocks again and again in utter frustration. Left knee, right shin, struggling forward, until I swim hands first into a razor-sharp rock, enough is enough!

"You won't get me! …You will not defeat me! …You hear me! …I will make it!"

Out of breath I roar at the rocks, mountains, and just about everything that tries to break me without success.

"I'm fighting back, you hear me!" I had enough of nature's round-the-clock attacks. I will rather lose my head before losing my mind, I decided.

"We made it, you didn't drown." I gratefully exclaimed, dragging my backpack out of the water onto the riverbed.

"You will cause my death…"

"…If we find a river again, what will I do with you?" I look at my drenched backpack soaked like a sponge, wondering how we made it through.

"A little moldy, hey." I nibble on my last piece of wet biltong to regain some strength for the day.

"Mm, my last food." That piece is just enough to make me realize how hungry I really am.

"Thank you Lord for protecting me. Help me to come out alive…I beg you dear Lord, amen."

"How did I not kick the bucket yet?" I realize that it was only by the grace of God.

Ready with my wet backpack on my shoulders, I started searching again for the mysterious path to survival along the winding Knysna River. According to intuition, I believed it must have been just above me over the mountain, but with no way out of the maze, I had to continue climbing over washed-up trees and boulders as far as the flow of the river allowed me.

The peaceful tranquility of the diverse 'worlds' that the Knysna forest possesses carried me away in all its splendor.

I am sure it was a bushbuck or a rabbit that darted off in the distance through the branches. There was such a wide variety of Fauna and Flora in absolute harmony around me that caused a sense of peace, freedom, and fulfillment to flood over me. I was tired, hungry, and hurt, but this fairy-tale world reminded me of the reason why I came back for another hike.

As the blistering sun found a way to burst through the roof of the treetops, I wondered what hour it was.

"Maybe, twelve o'clock?" My unbeatable inner clock reassured me that there was still sufficient time in the day to surprise my mates before dusk.

*"Dear Lord, please don't let me be lost for another day.
Let me get out of here safely, amen."*

As the river started flowing with faster and stronger intensity, I was brought back to reality as concerns began giving me the creeps. It was evident that if I were to spend another night in the forest I would not be able to sleep warm, next to a fire with dry clothes and a full stomach.

"Tonight, you are at the hut, I promise." I successfully silenced my concern with empty promises.

Space has drastically reduced, and moving on forced me to be more daring over huge rocks.

"Wow, safe! Not again, please." At last the riverbed became wider and more favorable to walk in. To my amazement, a few feet away, a beautiful parrot sat on a branch almost next to me. It was an incredible sight, where you almost couldn't believe what you saw, because where in my life have I ever seen a beautiful parrot in the wild and not in a cage?

"It probably escaped," I smiled. The beautiful shades of the parrot's colors were like an injection of motivation.

"I will make it, woo-hoo, I will make it…"

I immediately decided it had to be a sign or something. I was in a positive mood and ready again for anything. It was almost as if nature had listened to my eruption earlier in the day. The river and stones were favorable again and allowed me to walk freely over all obstacles without shoves, blows, or bumps.

"Oh, dear Jesus, help me Lord, please help me find the way back again, amen."

The thought of having to catch food if I spent another day in the woods, made me scratch my head a little.

"You will make it. Tonight, you are at the hut." I fought courageously against losing hope, but after so many hours, I still was not able to get out of the river's stronghold. I continued to diminish the minutes under my feet with my mindless "when I'm finally out of here" game, but inside I was clueless as to how I would ever get out.

Suddenly, life-changing hope spilled over me. I almost cried with happiness when I notice a few burnt logs.

"People were here before, people were here before!"

"Yes." The fat on that old logs asserts that someone has definitely braaied [roasted] meat here.

"Cold…warm…warmer…" I realize that I need to be very close to a hiking trail because people will not make a fire too far off the beaten track.

"Unless they got lost too…" I stop my joy from causing another disappointment.

Attentively, I searched with my eyes, focused on any signs of a hiking trail carefully to avoid any animal trails.

"Scorching…you're burning! You are burning!" I suddenly freeze like a television without a signal, dead in my tracks until I realize that my eyes are not deceiving me.

"H-e-y! …H-e-y!" For all I am worth, I scream at the top of my lungs at a group of people who fetched water from the river a few hundred meters away.

"Stop! Stop… I…" I run as fast as I can, staggering, towards the group of people who have since turned to look at me in amazement.

"…Got lost…" I drop breathlessly to my haunches and stare at the group in bewilderment.

"Ah… is that you?" The boy's eyes widen in disbelief.

"We thought you were already dead, bro everyone is looking for you! Sir… Sir… Look who I found?"

As I walk with the boy to their group, I notice that they too have gone off the road to fill their water bottles.

[Imagine the miracle of God's perfect timing. How is it even possible? If they stayed on the road and had not stopped at the river for that moment, I would have probably carried on down the winding river deeper into the heart of the Knysna River for days. But Jesus had a different plan.]

"You must be hungry?" The friendly man gave me a cold piece of meat while taking out his cell phone.

"You can relax here. I'm going to make a quick call."

"I actually have to catch up with my group. Do you know where…?"

I wanted to explain that I was about a day behind my group and that I desperately needed to catch up, but to no avail.

"You stay here, we will be walking in a group, shortly." I had no choice but to join the group.

I walked past the girls who chew with great curiosity, to where I found a big rock where I started to carefully unpack my backpack.

'Okay, I probably don't smell that fresh…? Don't look at me like that!' One by one I hang my soaked, dirty clothes in the cold sun. Meanwhile, interestingly, I chew on the piece of grilled meat with no appetite.

"Yes…we found Cornelius, just after 14:00 pm…yes, he's safe. …I'll relay the message…"

I am slightly dejected because I actually found them and not the other way around.

"Hey you, what happened?" A young girl curiously asks while chewing non-stop on a Bar-One.

As I realized how I could do with one of those twenty-five-hour days chocolate bars, I told her my abridged version of all the dangers, I faced.

"Woah…no way! Really?"

It was as if everyone in the choir appreciated how blessed I was to be alive.

"Dude, that's sick timing." I nodded.

The reaction of everyone's 'ooh' and 'aahs' to my wounds was interrupted by the call of my name.

"Cornelius, they are on their way. They will get you at the main road." I agree with perplexed wonder.

"Who's fetching me? How does he know my name? How do they know so much about me?"

"Five minutes." At the command of 'Mr.in-charge', everyone packs away to be ready again.

I suddenly remember that my damp clothes are still hanging from the branches.

'Aye…it's foul anyway.' I bundle my clothes carefully into my backpack. I wanted to finish my race without the help of anyone.

It was well deserving after all the hardship and pain I endured.

'So close…' on command, I take my place in the middle of the group.

"Peter, make sure that Cornelius doesn't fall behind." I was so misjudged, walking with a few guys in front and behind me on the way back to the hiking trail.

'I'm not so pathetic…I actually have the best direction…I'm the king of the forest!'

I swallowed my pride and moved on. I wanted to show everyone that I only made a small judgment error, but in the end found the way.

'Ah…here you are. So easy.' The footpath made its appearance, and in full glory, simultaneously stripped me from all my words.

'I was right, I was right! I knew the road was up this mountain.' I justify my frustrations in silence.

The heights along the Knysna River elicited almost painful memories and emotions as we strolled on the beautiful path that was so enjoyable up the mountain.

'Everything is so easy now.' Memories of those thorny branches that hurt my ribs almost made me smile.

When the six-kilometer sign appeared, I was overcome with a sense of humility.

"Only six." My heart suddenly caused painful, frustrating shock waves when I noticed a familiar sight below.

'There I climbed over the dangerous rocks this morning…there I battled through the river…' the painful live stream on repeat, dragged my emotions back in time.

'That's where I slept last night…'

I did not know how to respond to my sensory overload when I realized that I literally slept below the road to 'salvation.'

'I was so close…so close!' I holistically snug back into my world, not being able to process head from tail of my unsettled feelings in silence.

'Another day in the woods… yes…?' The path swung to the right, protecting me from any further painful mementos.

'I couldn't climb the cliff anyway' I attempted to justify my choices.

The steep, lush green mountain trail next to my flashback turned downhill onto the main road, where a forester and his bakkie [pickup truck] were waiting for us. After graciously thanking the group, I climbed into the back of the bakkie, and it almost felt like I was in the back of a police vehicle.

I kept waving to the group until the winding road made it impossible for anyone to be seen. In the back of the bakkie, I was tossed painfully back and forth on the rocky road like the multitude of my thoughts seeking answers to my rhetorical questions.

Through the bakkie's small rear window, I pondered in reverence how a beautiful, majestic forest such as this could evoke such eerie, unsteady-charming, and bittersweet memories.

'What will I say to my group when I see them again?' 'How will I be received?'

I was bombarded by the never-ending zigzag of the beautiful path.

'What does it look like, Sparky-the-Knysna-king could not finish the route himself?' The truck approached the destination, almost slanderous.

With its screeching brakes down the descent, it reminded me of that characterful amusing baboon, and I chuckled.

"Oh, what an adventure!" The well-known Diepwalle [*Deep walls – referring to the high cliffs*] hut makes its appearance.

"Unbelievable…gosh, I'm a machine." I realize that I nearly finished three hikes in one.

"Your direction is superb." I arrive absolutely delighted without a map, safe at my destination.

"Last time, within three hours, this time…within three days." I smiled. Sweet memories reminded me of how I was the 'Knysna-masseuse' last time at this hut.

I climbed harum-scarum, unassisted from the bakkie, not seeing a soul in sight, and greeted the ranger benignly.

"Thank you so much for everyone's effort." I approach the group a little concerned not knowing how they will respond.

"Speedy! Speedy … come here!" I was about to surprise the group, but was first overwhelmed by a very excited Mrs. Grobler.

"Speedy, what was it like being alone in the woods?" "Where did you sleep last night?"

"Are you hurt?"

I wanted to say something, but I did not get a chance. "Everyone … Speedy is here! Speedy is here!" I smile at my wonderfully ironic nickname.

Thank you to Mrs. Grobler's big voice, I am greeted with mixed reactions from the group.

"We're so glad nothing happened to you, Sparky." A group of girls kindly welcome me back, while other guys in passing, attempt to make a mockery of me in a high-pitched tone.

"Yeah, Sparky … so scared last night, you peed yourself."

"…Help Daddy, help, I'm so lost."

As the guys sarcastically scoffed and laughed, trying to re-enact my quandary, I could not care less because I survived.

'Wonder where's my 'Knysna girl' hiding?' Again Mrs. Grobler approached me.

"Cornelius, your father is almost here … they are coming from Cape Town."

After apologizing and explaining why I had to break her golden rules without intention, I approached the outside fire that was burning so blissfully. Once again, I reminisced how I lay peacefully by the fire on that rocky surface next to the river.

'I had no time to be frightened.' With joy I realize that I was so focused on survival that I forgot to be afraid.

Enchanted by the warm flames of the tranquil fire, suddenly a soft, tender hand touches my shoulder, and my eyes begin to light up. Expectant, almost sure of whom that hand should belong to, I turn, toward the warmest, most meaningful embrace of my 'Knysna blossom.'

"I was so worried." She whispered softly in my ear as I received the hug of a lifetime.

"I didn't close my eyes last night, Sparky…I was so worried."

"The ranger said you were definitely cat food…we all prayed for you." I saw that it really upset her.

"Hey…sweet Nicky…" I was totally taken aback to see how much she cared while my heart pounded recklessly.

"Gosh, I have to get lost more often." I smile teasingly.

[How much pain will a man endure to be happy? I am not going to lie, that hug was incredible yet slightly painful.]

"No, I…I don't hurt at all…old wounds." I reassured her through my teeth that those wounds seemed worse than they really are.

Snuggling up next to each other at the fire, I opened up about that horrible mountain, my 'spray-can fire', that silly baboon, and how mesmerizingly pretty the stars shone through the treetops. It was absolutely enchanting, talking to her while swept away. She was so amiably adorable while we laughed non-stop at each other playfully.

Out of the blue, she lovingly touched my hands while her eyes and fingers inspected my wounds emphatically.

I wondered if it was just an excuse to touch my hands, but I was far too enthralled to care.

Gently she bit her lower lip as her glittering eyes carefully moved up from my hands, over my chin and nose until our eyes met captivatingly.

"I'm so glad you're safe, Sparky!" With every word from her heart, her eyes locked onto mine.

Her beautiful bright glowing eyes, her mouth so serious as she concentrated, and her captivating look that tantalized me so fiercely, I stumbled in my quest to act normally.

"Unbelievable, how unpredictable life is…" I explained to my 'Knysna-girl' with sweet surrender that just earlier in the day, I battled through the deep, dark waters of the forest and now only a few hours later, I am sitting here…next to her by the fire.

Her dreams and goals were revealed to me, and I gave her permission that one day if I am really hurt she may examine me.

As the world stood still between us, with plenty on our hearts, we were cut short like before.

"Cornelius, your parents are here." Mrs. Grobler announced that my shortened hike unfortunately ended.

Immediately, I take a picture of my group so that I could at least have a memory of everyone that was part of my great excursion.

[Guess who 'Knysna-blossom' is.]

With a quick 'goodbye' to my group and one last tight hug-moment between 'Knysna girl' and me, I met my anxious family.

A final "Thank you, Mrs. Grobler," and a goodbye wave through the rear window of the moving car allowed the miles to become more and more, and I quieter.

The dusty gravel through the majestic forest slowly turned into a wide asphalt road.

At the same time, my mom listened to the 5:30 p.m. news on her favorite radio station.

As my surroundings changed, I stared wide-eyed at the informal settlement with its sink shacks built on the edge of the forest.

'Oh …I did not think I would see that again.'

Everything was just too vast, too much, too fast, and I almost too temperamental. I was hungry, and even though my parents bought me something to eat, I could not think about eating.

I yearned back to the turmoil of the forest, somewhere where I could disappear and be friends with my emotions, all alone and not overwhelmed by everything.

Almost halfway through the 1492km [±1000mile] journey back to Rustenburg, in the Northwest Province, I opened up.

After laughing at the silly fall and trying to help my 'Knysna girl' with noble intentions, I finally told a shortened version of my epic adventure to my family.

"Wow…really, aunt Dalene cried so much?"

"…A whole group of people prayed non-stop across South Africa, because of Mom?"

It was overwhelmingly reassuring to know how many people care about me.

"I should write a book…? Christiaan, you're so funny." I laughed at my big brother's ridiculous idea, because where would Sparky buy such heroism?

Calmly, I stared at the flashing headlights of the cars, reminiscing of the majestic grandeur of the forest, the hardship, dangers, friendly ghosts, extraordinary animals, and my adorable 'Knysna-blossom.'

My mind was filled with hopeful, exciting scenarios of how we might meet again. At peace, I continued gazing at the reflection of her mesmerizing, shimmering, smiling, eyes in the bright heavens over the Karoo.

That night I promised myself, with no need to rush, that when she studies medicine, I would finally get my girl.

Relieved with my outcome, I could hardly wait to tell my epic adventure to Mielies, my doggy.

Wrapped cozily in my serene thoughts, I realized, for the first time, that I was completely healed from that silly adventurous craving of 'getting lost in the Knysna forest.'

As I relived a few entertaining, nostalgic moments, I grimace slightly daringly:

"Well, maybe until next year…"

The End

Sparky's Last Thoughts

In hindsight, I realized that all my prayers had unknowingly came true. It was awe-inspiring when I realized how Christ Jesus helped me through the clutches of death. I should have died, but I did not. I realized that God has a humongous plan for my life, and so does He for yours. He loves you and cares for you.

In Jeremiah 29:11-13 [NIV] God says;

"11 For I know the plans I have for you, declares the Lord, plans to prosper you and not to harm you, plans to give you hope and a future. 12 Then you will call on me and come and pray to me, and I will listen to you. 13 You will seek me and find me when you seek me with all your heart."

Throughout the journey, I wanted God to fix my mistakes instantly. I wanted God to send angels to pick me up and fly me back to safety. I desperately sought a way out instead of seeing the miracle of God's love behind it. Overwhelmed at the mountain in my way, I should have had faith, walking with confidence that God has already worked it out.

"And we know that all things work together for good to those who love God, to those who are the called according to His purpose." Romans 8:28.

Through the overwhelming anxiety, the hurt, the scars, and even a place of certain death, Jesus was with me every step of the way.

When my body became too weak, He strengthened me, and with His perfect timing, He positioned me and my surroundings to work out perfectly.

In the end, I not only found safety but a greater revelation of how deeply, caring, and loving our God really is. Always remember that no matter what you are faced with and no matter how impossible it may seem, God will provide a real solution at His perfect time – the best time for you. When your storms feel too big to handle, they probably are. That is why we need to give our storms to Jesus and let Him calm them for us. We are not created to try and face up to all life throws at us, it will just weigh us down and burden us.

"28 Come to me, all you who are weary and burdened, and I will give you rest. 29 Take my yoke upon you and learn from me, for I am gentle and humble in heart, and you will find rest for your souls. 30 For my yoke is easy and my burden is light." Matthew 11:28-30 [NIV]

God specializes in making the impossible, possible. Just trust in Him, He will make a way where there is no way. He will give you peace.

"And the peace of God, which surpasses all understanding, will guard your hearts and your minds in Christ Jesus." Philippians 4:7

Be blessed. Love, Sparky.

How to Cheat Death
(and get away with it)

You have reached the end of my first story in the series 'The Adventures of Sparky – Knysna Forest'. The following is only for the brave and the real adventurers. You do not need to read the following. So please close this book now.

If you haven't closed the book and you are still reading, I want to commend you for your bravery. Are you sure you want to know how to cheat death?

Dear________________________,

[Your name]

What is today's date? Remember it. The following might shock you. Death is already dead. Say it with me loud. Death is dead! Death had a funeral. It was very sad. Some of us still don't want to accept the fact that death died long ago and are still trying to befriend death.

"Hey, death, let's take a selfie together."

Death lost its sting when Jesus defeated death more than 2000 years ago. Because Jesus died on the cross and rose from the dead, we can be with Him forever in heaven if that is what we choose. When we trust in Jesus, we enter into a personal, permanent relationship with God and as a result we have eternal life. When we allow Jesus to live in our hearts, we will never ever be the same again.

Don't look at religion; religion will tell you there is a way to earn your way into heaven. Look at Jesus.

Jesus is the way and the truth and the life, and no one comes to the Father except through Jesus. John 14:6 [NIV]

Jesus loves you. Even If you don't believe it, He really does. Maybe even your mamma does not love you like she used to, because you did something a little horrendous. Jesus still loves you. Say it with me loud. Jesus loves me. Say it again.

Jesus loves________________,

[Your name]

Come on, say it like you mean it. This is the best news ever.

*Jesus loves*________________,
[Your name]

That's better. Maybe this is the most difficult thing to believe, since [let's face it, sometimes you don't even love yourself] we have a few things that we are not so proud of. Things that we are ashamed of, and would rather die than let our friends and family find out what we are hiding from the world. If we are honest, there are some things we tried to get rid of in the past and lost count so many times we tried to stop doing it.

But it keeps on coming back, again and again, and again. You know what I mean. The struggle is real people. If you are sick and tired of losing that same battle again and again, then maybe it is time to change your strategy. Do something new – something that will work.

So, everyone, reading this from your beautifully decorated prison cell, I am not talking now about 'Lockdown.'

If you feel like you are trapped by your past, or stuck in a spiral with the same habits that started impacting or affecting your life negatively, then I am here to give you hope.

I know a friend called Jesus, and I am super excited to tell you about my best friend. I can call him a friend because I have gotten to know him on a personal level just before this miracle experience about 17 years ago. He is the answer to destroying all your struggles. He will fight your battle if you let Him.

So, all these habits that we all know lead to death, eternal death, and I am not here to scare you. You are probably still recovering from my Knysna Forest experience. I am here to bring you hope and super amazing news that there is freedom from all your struggles. Here's my question to you; *Do you feel overwhelmed and maybe struggle with anxiety, depression, addictions, and sometimes feel like giving up on life?* You can find freedom today. You might ask me:

"Sparky, how do I find freedom?"

The only way to find freedom is to give all your struggles to Jesus, He will set you free.

Look at the following illustrations: The self-directed life versus the Christ-directed life. Which one best describes you?

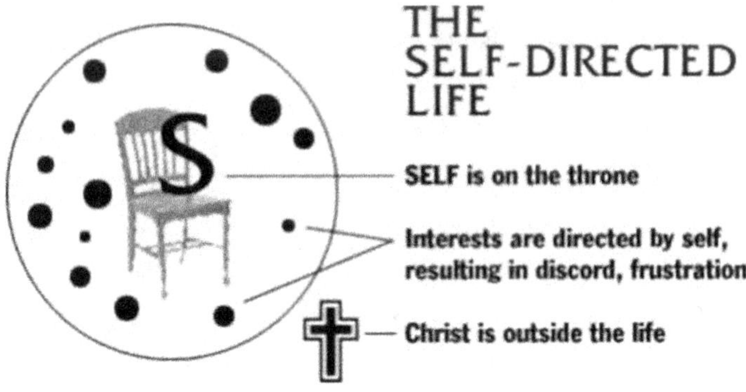

As you can see, when we direct our own life we end up fighting a losing battle, and it will feel as if everything is against us. The result is frustration, and our lives and relationships will be negatively impacted.

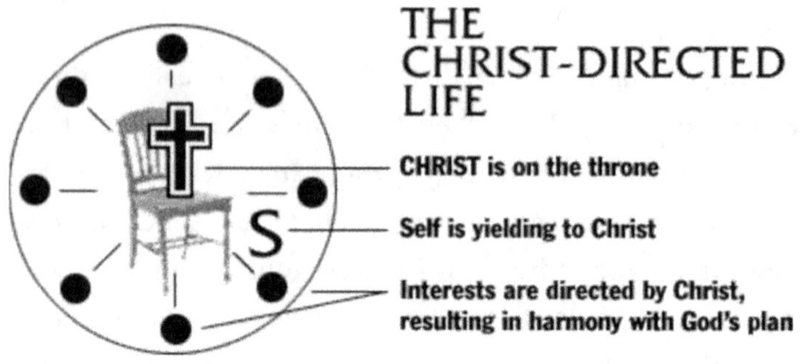

http://www.4laws.com/laws/englishkgp/default.htm

The Christ-directed life is the safest space. It is the place where you can relax in God's freedom, knowing that God is working out all your struggles.

He promised you a hope and a future, and when we allow Christ to direct our lives, we receive love, joy, peace, patience, kindness, goodness, faithfulness, gentleness, and self-control as promised in Galatians 5:22-23 in the Bible.

So friend, there is hope and freedom in Christ. Let Him break your chains today and let Him give you a new heart. Why don't you destroy the power that death has over you? Death is already defeated, so why would you live in defeat when you can be victorious in Christ Jesus? Give your heart and life to Jesus.

Quiet your heart for a moment. God loves you and has been waiting for you all along. He wants to remove your past now. He is at the door of your heart, and he is whispering your name.

Come to me_______________, I love you, my child, I have been so excited for you to meet me before you were born. I am so proud of you, my child. You are trying so hard to be good. And I see all your efforts. My child, you don't have to try so hard.

Just come to me and find peace. I want to show you how much I love you. I loved you even before you were formed in your mother's womb.

I have known you even before the foundations of this earth were laid, I know what you need, and I will provide for you.

I know every heartache, every tear, every struggle, and every defeat every time you fell short of my glory, but I want to help you, and I want to take the pain away from you, my child.

I want to give you a new heart. I want to give you a new life. I want to provide you with joy, my child. Let me help you carry the weight, it is too heavy for you my child. I am not mad at you my child. I want to be the best, loving Father you have ever known. Please let me. Come and speak to your Father, my child. Come pray to me.

Dear God,

Thank you for Jesus. God, I know I am a sinner, please forgive me for all my sins. Thank you Jesus that you have died on the cross for me. Thank you that your blood washed away all my sins, and at this moment I am now forgiven. Every sin I have committed is now washed clean by the precious blood of Jesus. I want to know you Lord, I want to commit my life to you. Holy Spirit, please come into my heart and change me inside out.

Make me new, restore me, and give me a brand-new heart. Now in the mighty name of Jesus, I break every chain in my life. I am loved by Jesus. I am forgiven.

Thank you Jesus, for the strength and courage to turn away from all my sins.

Thank you Lord, that you are now my Father. Please show me how much you love me, fill me up entirely with your Spirit. Thank you Father, that one day I will meet you in Heaven. I am set free, I am forgiven, and I am born again.

Amen.

"If you declare with your mouth, "Jesus is Lord," and believe in your heart that God raised him from the dead, you will be saved." Romans 10:9[NIV]

CONGRATULATIONS

IT IS OFFICIAL – YOU BELONG TO GOD

Date: _____________________.

This is to certify that____________________, is a born-again
believer and on this day accepted
Jesus Christ as our Lord and Savior.

*I tell you that in the same way there will be more rejoicing in
Heaven over one sinner who repents than over ninety-nine
righteous persons who do not need to repent. Luke 15:7 [NIV]*

Happy Birthday Fellow Believer

Dear brother/sister in Christ. We are now family and I am overjoyed by your decision to follow Jesus. You will not regret this day, I promise. Remember this day, because life will never be the same again. Your real, incredible, exciting adventure starts now. It is your new birthday, so it is time to celebrate! Don't celebrate alone. Go and tell the world what Jesus has done for you. You are now a child of God.

www.ingramcontent.com/pod-product-compliance
Lightning Source LLC
Chambersburg PA
CBHW071331150726
47997CB00002B/682